Favorite Brand Name

SLOW COOKER RECIPES

Contents

main-dish **meats**

Swiss Steak

Amy Rivera / Arlington, VA

1 onion, sliced into thick rings
1 clove garlic, minced
1 beef round steak (2 pounds), cut to fit into slow cooker
All-purpose flour
Salt
Black pepper
1 can (28 ounces) whole tomatoes, undrained
1 can (10¾ ounces) condensed tomato soup, undiluted
3 medium potatoes, unpeeled, diced
1 package (16 ounces) frozen peas and carrots
1 cup sliced celery
Additional vegetables

1. Place onion and garlic in bottom of slow cooker.

2. Dredge steak in flour seasoned with salt and pepper. Shake off excess flour. Place steak in slow cooker. Add tomatoes with juice. Cover with tomato soup. Add potatoes, peas and carrots, celery and any additional vegetables. Cover; cook on HIGH 4 to 6 hours or until meat and potatoes are tender.

Makes 8 servings

Amy says: I sometimes add corn or green beans. This recipe is very easy and definitely a family favorite!

Swiss Steak

Honey Ribs

Donna Urbanek / Levittown, PA

1 can (10¾ ounces) condensed beef consommé, undiluted
½ cup water
3 tablespoons soy sauce
2 tablespoons honey
2 tablespoons maple syrup
2 tablespoons barbecue sauce
½ teaspoon dry mustard
2 pounds extra-lean baby back ribs

1. Combine all ingredients except ribs in slow cooker; mix well.

2. Add ribs to slow cooker. (If ribs are especially fatty, broil 10 minutes before adding to slow cooker.) Cover; cook on LOW 6 to 8 hours or on HIGH 4 hours or until ribs are tender. *Makes 4 servings*

Donna says: These ribs are delicious alone, but are even better served with rice.

Chili Verde

Pam Egendorfer / Newbury Park, CA

1 tablespoon vegetable oil
1 to 2 pounds boneless pork chops
Sliced carrots (enough to cover bottom of slow cooker)
1 jar (24 ounces) mild green chili salsa
Chopped onion (optional)

1. Heat oil in large skillet over medium-low heat. Brown pork on both sides. Drain excess fat.

2. Place carrot slices in bottom of slow cooker. Place pork on top of carrots. Pour salsa over chops. Add onion to taste, if desired. Cover; cook on HIGH 6 to 8 hours.

Pam says: If desired, shred the pork and serve it with tortillas.
Makes 4 to 8 servings

Honey Ribs

Smothered Beef Patties

Carol Occhipinti / Fort Worth, TX

Worcestershire sauce
Garlic powder
Salt
Black pepper
1 can (14½ ounces) Mexican-style diced tomatoes with green chilies, undrained, divided
8 frozen beef patties, unthawed
1 onion, cut into 8 slices

Sprinkle bottom of slow cooker with small amount of Worcestershire sauce, garlic powder, salt, pepper and 2 tablespoons tomatoes. Add 1 frozen beef patty. Top with Worcestershire sauce, garlic powder, salt, pepper, 2 tablespoons tomatoes and 1 onion slice. Repeat layers. Cover; cook on LOW 8 hours. *Makes 8 servings*

Carol says: Serve these patties with mashed potatoes and a Caesar salad. They are also delicious with steamed rice.

So Simple Supper!

Charlotte Walker / Richmond, VA

1 beef chuck shoulder roast (3 to 4 pounds)
1 package (1 ounce) dry onion soup mix
1 package (1 ounce) mushroom gravy mix
1 package (1 ounce) au jus gravy mix
3 cups water
Assorted vegetables (potatoes, carrots, onions and celery)

1. Place roast in slow cooker. Combine soup and gravy mixes and water in large bowl. Pour mixture over roast. Cover; cook on LOW 4 hours.

2. Add vegetables. Cover; cook 2 more hours or until meat and vegetables are tender. *Makes 8 servings*

Smothered Beef Patty

Slow Cooker Meatloaf

Carolyn Stanley / Middletown, DE

1½ pounds ground beef
¾ cup milk
⅔ cup fine dry bread crumbs
2 eggs, beaten
2 tablespoons minced onion
1 teaspoon salt
½ teaspoon ground sage
½ cup ketchup
2 tablespoons brown sugar
1 teaspoon dry mustard

1. Combine beef, milk, bread crumbs, eggs, onion, salt and sage in large bowl. Shape into ball and place in slow cooker. Cover; cook on LOW 5 to 6 hours.

2. Fifteen minutes before serving, combine ketchup, brown sugar and mustard in small bowl. Pour over meatloaf. Cover; cook on HIGH 15 minutes. *Makes 6 servings*

Carolyn says: This is so good, I serve it to company!

Fall Apart Pork Chops

Pat Ellis / Waynesville, NC

2 teaspoons vegetable oil
4 center-cut bone-in pork chops
1 can (10¾ ounces) condensed cream of mushroom soup, undiluted
¼ cup water
¼ cup cooking wine (sherry or marsala) or apple juice

1. Heat oil in large skillet over medium-low heat. Brown pork chops on both sides; season as desired. Drain excess fat. Transfer pork chops to slow cooker.

2. Whisk together soup, water and wine in large bowl. Pour mixture over pork. Cover; cook on HIGH 3 hours or until meat is tender. (Cook longer for very thick chops.) *Makes 4 servings*

Pat says: When this dish is ready to serve, the soup mixture will have made a nice gravy. Serve it over buttered noodles or rice. Enjoy!

Slow Cooker Meatloaf

Round Steak

Deborah Long / Bridgeport, CT

- 1 round steak (1½ pounds), trimmed and cut into 4 equal-size pieces
- ¼ cup all-purpose flour
- 1 teaspoon black pepper
- ½ teaspoon salt
- 1 tablespoon vegetable oil
- 1 can (10¾ ounces) condensed cream of mushroom soup, undiluted
- ¾ cup water
- 1 medium onion, quartered
- 1 can (4 ounces) sliced mushrooms, drained
- ¼ cup milk
- 1 package (1 ounce) dry onion soup mix
- Salt
- Black pepper
- Ground sage
- Dried thyme leaves
- 1 bay leaf

1. Place steaks in large resealable plastic food storage bag. Close bag and pound with meat mallet to tenderize.

2. Combine flour, pepper and salt in small bowl; add to bag with steaks. Shake to coat meat evenly.

3. Heat oil in large nonstick skillet. Remove steaks from bag; shake off excess flour. Add steaks to skillet; brown both sides.

4. Transfer steaks and pan juices to slow cooker. Add mushroom soup, water, onion, mushrooms, milk, dry onion soup mix, seasonings to taste, and bay leaf to slow cooker; mix well. Cover; cook on LOW 5 to 6 hours or until steak is tender. Remove and discard bay leaf before serving.

Makes 4 servings

Round Steak

Simply Delicious Pork

Carol Morris / Auburn, IN

1½ pounds boneless pork loin, sliced
4 medium Yellow Delicious apples, sliced
3 tablespoons brown sugar
1 teaspoon cinnamon
½ teaspoon salt

1. Place pork slices in bottom of slow cooker. Cover with apples.

2. Combine brown sugar, cinnamon and salt in small bowl; sprinkle over apples. Cover; cook on LOW 6 to 8 hours. *Makes 6 servings*

Slow-Cooked Beef Brisket Dinner

Marie McConnell / Las Cruces, NM

1 beef brisket (4 pounds), cut in half
4 to 6 medium potatoes, cut into large chunks
6 carrots, cut into 1-inch pieces
8 ounces mushrooms, sliced
½ large onion, sliced
1 rib celery, cut into 1-inch pieces
3 cubes beef bouillon
5 cloves garlic, crushed
1 teaspoon black peppercorns
2 bay leaves
Water

1. Place all ingredients in slow cooker. Add water to cover ingredients. Cover; cook on LOW 6 to 8 hours. Remove and discard bay leaves.

2. Remove brisket to cutting board. Slice meat across grain. Serve with vegetables. *Makes 8 to 10 servings*

Marie says: The meat will likely fall apart with slicing, but will be very tender and full of flavor. Slice the meat and serve it in large bowls with the vegetables. You can add the flavorful cooking juices to the bowls and serve crusty bread for dipping. (Be sure to first strain the juices to remove the garlic and peppercorns.)

Simply Delicious Pork

Autumn Delight

Regina Hill / Burnsville, NC

4 to 6 beef cubed steaks
Olive oil
2 to 3 cans (10¾ ounces each) condensed cream of mushroom soup, undiluted
1 to 1½ cups water
1 package (1 ounce) dry onion soup mix or mushroom soup mix

1. Lightly brown cubed steaks in oil in large nonstick skillet over medium heat. Place steaks in slow cooker.

2. Add soup, water (½ cup water per can of soup) and soup mix to slow cooker; stir to combine. Cover; cook on LOW 4 to 6 hours.

Makes 4 to 6 servings

Regina says: This is a wonderfully easy entrée. Enjoy!

Curried Pork Pot

Gina Brittain / Schenectady, NY

1 can (10¾ ounces) condensed cream of chicken soup, undiluted
1 cup evaporated skimmed milk or water
1 medium onion, chopped
½ cup raisins
1 tablespoon mild curry powder
1 tablespoon dried parsley flakes
1 teaspoon minced garlic
1 pound boneless country-style pork ribs
Salt
Black pepper
Hot cooked rice, pasta or egg noodles

1. Combine soup, milk, onion, raisins, curry powder, parsley and garlic in large bowl; mix well. Add pork; stir to coat.

2. Place mixture in slow cooker. Cover; cook on LOW 6 to 8 hours or on HIGH 4 to 6 hours. Stir in salt and pepper to taste. Serve over rice, pasta or noodles.

Makes 6 servings

Autumn Delight

Hearty Calico Bean Dip

Heather Daoust / Ashland, WI

¾ pound ground beef
½ pound sliced bacon, crisp-cooked and crumbled
1 can (16 ounces) baked beans
1 can (15½ ounces) Great Northern beans, rinsed and drained
1 can (15½ ounces) kidney beans, rinsed and drained
1 small onion, chopped
½ cup brown sugar
½ cup ketchup
1 tablespoon vinegar
1 teaspoon prepared yellow mustard
Tortilla chips

1. Brown ground beef in medium skillet, stirring to break up meat; drain. Place meat in slow cooker.

2. Add remaining ingredients except tortilla chips to slow cooker; stir to combine. Cover; cook on LOW 4 hours or on HIGH 2 hours. Serve with tortilla chips. Garnish as desired. *Makes 12 servings*

Heather says: Place in serving dish, and scoop up dip with tortilla chips.

Simple Slow Cooker Pork Roast

Andrea Shuster / Plantsville, CT

4 to 5 red potatoes, cut into bite-size pieces
4 carrots, cut into bite-size pieces
1 marinated pork roast (3 to 4 pounds)
½ cup water
1 package (10 ounces) frozen baby peas
Salt
Black pepper

Place potatoes, carrots and roast in slow cooker. Add water. Cover; cook on LOW 6 to 8 hours or until vegetables are tender. Add peas during last hour of cooking. Season to taste with salt and pepper.

Makes 6 servings

Hearty Calico Bean Dip

Beef Roll-Ups

Mary Schrank / Racine, WI

1 beef round steak (1½ pounds), ½ inch thick
4 slices bacon
½ cup diced green bell pepper
¼ cup diced onion
¼ cup diced celery
1 can (10 ounces) beef gravy

1. Cut steak into 4 pieces. Place 1 bacon slice on each piece.

2. Combine bell pepper, onion, and celery in medium bowl. Place about ¼ cup mixture on each piece of meat. Roll up meat; secure with wooden toothpicks.

3. Place beef rolls in slow cooker. Pour gravy evenly over top. Cover; cook on LOW 8 to 10 hours. Skim fat; discard. *Makes 4 servings*

Mary says: Serve with mashed potatoes or over rice.

Ham & Potato Scallop

Carol Taylor / Millington, MD

8 slices ham
1 large onion, sliced
4 medium potatoes, thinly sliced
Salt
Black pepper
1 cup corn
1 can (10¾ ounces) condensed cream of mushroom soup, undiluted
1 cup shredded Cheddar cheese
1 tablespoon Worcestershire sauce

1. Layer ham, onion and potatoes in slow cooker; season with salt and pepper. Add corn.

2. Combine soup, cheese and Worcestershire sauce in medium bowl. Pour over ham mixture. Cover; cook on LOW 8 hours or until potatoes are tender. *Makes 8 servings*

Beef Roll-Up

Smothered Steak

Edye Vanhouten / Fort Wayne, IN

1½ to 2 pounds beef cubed steak, cut into 4 pieces
All-purpose flour
1 can (10¾ ounces) condensed cream of mushroom soup, undiluted
1 package (1 ounce) dry onion soup mix

1. Dust steak lightly with flour. Place in slow cooker.

2. Combine mushroom soup and onion soup mix in medium bowl. Pour over steak. Cover; cook on LOW 6 to 8 hours. Serve over seasoned rice, if desired. *Makes 4 servings*

Edye says: It cooks all day for dinner tonight!

Buck County Ribs

Leonard Cranston / Westland, MI

4 boneless country-style pork ribs
1 teaspoon salt
1 jar (about 28 ounces) sauerkraut, drained
1 medium apple, diced
1 tablespoon sugar
1 cup chicken broth or 1 cup water plus 1 teaspoon chicken bouillon granules
Mashed potatoes (optional)

1. Place ribs in slow cooker. Sprinkle with salt.

2. Spoon sauerkraut over ribs. Top with apple. Sprinkle sugar over apple. Add chicken broth. Cover; cook on LOW 8 to 9 hours. Serve with mashed potatoes, if desired. *Makes 4 servings*

Smothered Steak

poultry entrées

French Country Slow Cooker Chicken

Teri Lindquist / Gurnee, IL

1 medium onion, chopped
4 carrots, sliced
4 ribs celery, sliced
6 to 8 boneless skinless chicken breasts (about 1½ to 2 pounds)
1 teaspoon dried tarragon leaves
1 teaspoon dried thyme leaves
Salt
Black pepper
1 can (10¾ ounces) condensed cream of chicken soup, undiluted
1 package (1 ounce) dry onion soup mix
⅓ cup white wine or apple juice
2 tablespoons cornstarch
Hot cooked rice (optional)

1. Place onion, carrots and celery in bottom of slow cooker. Arrange chicken over vegetables. Sprinkle with tarragon, thyme, salt and pepper.

2. Pour soup over chicken. Sprinkle with onion soup mix. Cover; cook on HIGH 3 to 4 hours, stirring once during cooking.

3. Twenty minutes before serving, whisk together wine and cornstarch in small bowl until smooth. Pour mixture over chicken; stir well. Cook, uncovered, on HIGH 15 minutes or until sauce thickens. Serve over rice, if desired.

Makes 6 to 8 servings

French Country Slow Cooker Chicken

Cheesy Slow Cooker Chicken

Joan VandenNoven / Beloit, WI

6 boneless skinless chicken breasts (about 1½ pounds)
Salt
Black pepper
Garlic powder
2 cans (10¾ ounces each) condensed cream of chicken soup, undiluted
1 can (10¾ ounces) condensed Cheddar cheese soup, undiluted
Chopped fresh parsley (optional)

1. Place 3 chicken breasts in slow cooker. Sprinkle with salt, pepper and garlic powder. Repeat with remaining three breasts and seasonings.

2. Combine soups in medium bowl; pour over chicken. Cover; cook on LOW 6 to 8 hours. Garnish with parsley before serving, if desired.

Makes 6 servings

Joan says: The sauce is wonderful over noodles, rice or mashed potatoes.

Sandy's Mexican Chicken

Sandra Sebesta / Lockhart, TX

2 chicken breasts (about ½ pound)
1 medium onion, sliced
1 can (10¾ ounces) condensed cream of chicken soup, undiluted
1 can (10 ounces) Mexican-style diced tomatoes with green chilies, undrained
1 package (8 ounces) American processed cheese food, cubed

1. Place all ingredients except cheese food in slow cooker. Cover; cook on LOW 6 to 8 hours or on HIGH 4 hours.

2. Break up chicken into pieces. Add cheese; cook on HIGH until melted.

Makes 2 to 4 servings

Sandra says: Serve over hot cooked spaghetti.

Cheesy Slow Cooker Chicken

Hot & Sour Chicken

Lynda McCormick / Burkburnett, TX

4 to 6 boneless skinless chicken breasts (about 1 to 1½ pounds)
1 package (1 ounce) dry hot-and-sour soup mix
1 cup chicken or vegetable broth

Place chicken in slow cooker. Add soup mix and broth. Cover; cook on LOW 5 to 6 hours. Garnish as desired. *Makes 4 to 6 servings*

Lynda says: This dish can be served over steamed white rice and topped with crispy Chinese noodles. Or, for a colorful variation, serve it over a bed of snow peas and sugar snap peas tossed with diced red bell pepper.

Bonnie's Slow-Cooked Turkey Thighs with Potatoes

Bonnie Luttrell / Bullhead City, AZ

1 large onion, sliced
2 turkey thighs, skin removed
2 cloves garlic, minced
½ teaspoon black pepper
8 to 10 small red potatoes
1 can (12 ounces) beer *or* 1½ cups chicken broth
1 can (8 ounces) tomato sauce
1 bay leaf

1. Place onion slices on bottom of slow cooker. Add turkey thighs; sprinkle with garlic and pepper.

2. Place potatoes around turkey thighs. Add beer, tomato sauce and bay leaf. Cover; cook on LOW 8 to 10 hours. Remove and discard bay leaf before serving. Makes 2 to 4 servings

Bonnie says: The meat will fall off the bones. It is great by itself or wrapped in tortillas.

Hot & Sour Chicken

Creamy Chicken and Mushrooms

Lisa Langston / Conroe, TX

1 teaspoon salt
½ teaspoon black pepper
¼ teaspoon paprika
3 boneless skinless chicken breasts, cubed
1½ cups sliced fresh mushrooms
½ cup sliced green onions
1¾ teaspoons chicken bouillon granules
1 cup dry white wine
½ cup water
1 can (5 ounces) evaporated milk
5 teaspoons cornstarch
Hot cooked rice

1. Combine salt, pepper and paprika in small bowl; sprinkle over chicken.

2. Layer chicken, mushrooms, green onions and bouillon in slow cooker. Pour wine and water over top. Cover; cook on HIGH 3 hours or on LOW 5 to 6 hours. Remove chicken and vegetables to platter; cover to keep warm.

3. Combine evaporated milk and cornstarch in small saucepan, stirring until smooth. Add 2 cups liquid from slow cooker; bring to a boil. Boil 1 minute or until thickened, stirring constantly. Serve chicken over rice and top with sauce. *Makes 3 to 4 servings*

Orange Chicken

Julie Vess / Camano Island, WA

4 boneless skinless chicken breasts (about 1 pound)
1 can (12 ounces) orange soda
½ cup soy sauce
Hot cooked rice

Place all ingredients except rice in slow cooker. Cover; cook on LOW 5 to 6 hours. Serve over rice. *Makes 4 servings*

Creamy Chicken and Mushrooms

Turkey Spaghetti Sauce

Sandra Glasson / Flushing, MI

1 tablespoon vegetable oil
2 pounds ground turkey
1 can (12 ounces) beer
1 jar (26 ounces) spaghetti sauce
Water
1 can (6 ounces) tomato paste
1 package (1½ ounces) dry spaghetti sauce seasoning mix

1. Heat oil in large skillet over medium-low heat. Add turkey; cook and stir until turkey is no longer pink. Add beer; cook and stir 2 to 3 minutes or until mixture is well combined.

2. Place turkey mixture in slow cooker. Add spaghetti sauce. Fill emptied sauce jar with water to rinse out remaining sauce; pour into slow cooker. Add tomato paste and seasoning mix; stir to combine. Cover; cook on LOW 6 to 8 hours. *Makes 8 servings*

Sandra says: I make this before I leave for work in the morning, and my children stir it when they get home from school. Then, when I get home from work, it's done!

Nice 'n' Easy Italian Chicken

Marcia Szczepaniak / Williamsville, NY

4 boneless skinless chicken breasts (about 1 pound)
8 ounces mushrooms, sliced
1 medium green bell pepper, chopped (optional)
1 medium zucchini, diced
1 medium onion, chopped
1 jar (26 ounces) spaghetti sauce

Combine all ingredients in slow cooker. Cover; cook on LOW 6 to 8 hours. *Makes 4 servings*

Marcia says: Serve over pasta of your choice.

My Favorite Chicken

MaryLou Rogers / Walla Walla, WA

1 whole chicken (about 3 pounds), cut into pieces
1 cup chopped onion
1 cup sliced celery
1 cup sliced carrots
½ teaspoon seasoning salt
½ teaspoon black pepper
¼ teaspoon garlic powder
¼ teaspoon poultry seasoning
3 to 4 medium potatoes, sliced
1 can (14 ounces) chicken broth

Place chicken pieces, onion, celery, carrots, seasoning salt, pepper, garlic powder and poultry seasoning in slow cooker. Top with potatoes. Pour broth over top. Cover; cook on HIGH 30 minutes. *Reduce heat to LOW;* cook 6 to 8 hours more. *Makes 4 servings*

MaryLou says: After cooking, use a slotted spoon to remove everything to a bowl. Thicken up the juice in the slow cooker with cornstarch and pour it into the serving bowl, as well.

Creamy Chicken

Debra Bowers / Manhattan, KS

3 boneless skinless chicken breasts *or* 6 boneless skinless chicken thighs
2 cans (10¾ ounces each) condensed cream of chicken soup, undiluted
1 can (14½ ounces) chicken broth
1 can (4 ounces) sliced mushrooms, drained
½ medium onion, diced
Salt
Black pepper

Place all ingredients in slow cooker. Cover; cook on LOW 6 to 8 hours. Season to taste with salt and pepper. *Makes 3 servings*

Debra says: If desired, add cubed American processed cheese food to the slow cooker before serving.

Heidi's Chicken Supreme

Kim Adams / Manchester, MO

1 can (10¾ ounces) condensed cream of chicken soup, undiluted
1 package (1 ounce) dry onion soup mix
6 boneless skinless chicken breasts (about 1½ pounds)
½ cup imitation bacon bits *or* ½ pound bacon, crisp-cooked and crumbled
1 container (16 ounces) reduced-fat sour cream

1. Spray inside of slow cooker with nonstick cooking spray. Combine soup with dry soup mix in medium bowl; mix well.

2. Layer chicken breasts and soup mixture in slow cooker. Sprinkle with bacon. Cover; cook on HIGH 4 hours or on LOW 8 hours. During last hour of cooking, stir in sour cream. *Makes 6 servings*

Kim says: This is delicious over noodles. You can also use condensed cream of mushroom soup or condensed cream of celery soup, if that is what you have on hand.

Gypsy's BBQ Chicken

Gypsy Heilman / Lawton, OK

6 boneless skinless chicken breasts (about 1½ pounds)
1 bottle (26 ounces) barbecue sauce
6 slices bacon
6 slices Swiss cheese

1. Place chicken in slow cooker. Cover with barbecue sauce. Cover; cook on LOW 8 to 9 hours.

2. Before serving, cut bacon slices in half. Cook bacon in microwave or on stove top, keeping bacon flat.

3. Place 2 slices cooked bacon over each piece of chicken in slow cooker. Top with cheese slices. Cover; cook on HIGH until cheese melts. *Makes 6 servings*

Gypsy says: If sauce becomes too thick during cooking, add a little water.

Heidi's Chicken Supreme

Continental Chicken

Helen Syfie / Omaha, NE

1 package (2¼ ounces) dried beef, cut up
4 boneless skinless chicken breasts (about 1 pound)
4 slices lean bacon
1 can (10¾ ounces) condensed cream of mushroom soup, undiluted
¼ cup all-purpose flour
¼ cup low-fat sour cream

1. Spray inside of slow cooker with nonstick cooking spray. Place dried beef in bottom of slow cooker. Wrap each piece of chicken with one bacon slice. Place wrapped chicken on top of dried beef.

2. Combine soup, flour and sour cream in medium bowl; mix until smooth. Pour over chicken. Cover; cook on LOW 7 to 9 hours or on HIGH 3 to 4 hours. *Makes 4 servings*

Helen says: Serve over hot buttered noodles.

Slow Cooker Turkey Breast

Bonnie Vezdos / Avon, OH

1 turkey breast (3 to 6 pounds)
Garlic powder
Paprika
Dried parsley flakes

Place turkey in slow cooker. Sprinkle with garlic powder, paprika and parsley to taste. Cover; cook on LOW 6 to 8 hours.

Makes 6 servings

Bonnie says: Don't add any liquid. The turkey makes its own juices.

Continental Chicken

Chicken and Stuffing

Anna Ertl / Franksville, WI

½ cup all-purpose flour
¾ teaspoon seasoned salt
¾ teaspoon black pepper
4 to 6 boneless skinless chicken breasts (about 1 to 1½ pounds)
¼ cup (½ stick) butter
2 cans (10¾ ounces each) condensed cream of mushroom soup, undiluted
1 package (12 ounces) seasoned stuffing mix, plus ingredients to prepare mix

1. Combine flour, seasoned salt and pepper in large resealable plastic food storage bag. Dredge chicken in flour mixture.

2. Melt butter in large skillet over medium-low heat. Brown chicken on both sides. Place in slow cooker. Pour soup over top.

3. Follow package directions for stuffing, decreasing liquid by half. Add stuffing to slow cooker over chicken. Cover; cook on HIGH 3 to 4 hours.

Makes 4 to 6 servings

Easy Slow Cooker Chicken and Gravy

Patricia Ogilsbie / Canastota, NY

1 can (10¾ ounces) condensed cream of chicken soup, undiluted
6 to 8 chicken legs, breast halves or assorted pieces
1 can (10¾ ounces) condensed cream of chicken Dijon soup *or* 1 can (10¾ ounces) condensed cream of chicken soup, undiluted

Pour 1 can chicken soup into slow cooker. Add chicken. Pour chicken Dijon soup over top. Cover; cook on LOW 8 to 10 hours.

Makes 6 servings

Patricia says: The soup makes a delicious gravy that can be served over pasta, rice or potatoes. For an added bonus, peel and chop a carrot and cook it along with the chicken.

Chicken and Stuffing

soups & stews

1-2-3-4 Chili

Carol Mason / Hanover Park, IL

2 pounds ground beef
4 cans (8 ounces each) tomato sauce
3 cans (15½ ounces each) chili beans in mild or spicy sauce, undrained
Shredded Cheddar cheese (optional)
Green onions, sliced (optional)

1. Cook beef in large skillet over medium-high heat until no longer pink, stirring often to separate meat; drain fat.

2. Add beef, tomato sauce and beans to slow cooker; stir to combine. Cover; cook on LOW 6 to 8 hours. Garnish with cheese and sliced green onions, if desired.

Makes 8 servings

Carol says: Just dump everything into your slow cooker. I set mine before I go to work, and I get to come home to a batch of (cheater) chili! It tastes great with cornbread, too.

Tip

Many variations of this thick, stewlike dish exist today. Chili's main ingredients are cubed or coarsely ground beef and chili peppers or chili powder. The addition of beans can be highly controversial with chili aficionados. While Texans generally do not add beans, others consider beans a necessity.

1-2-3-4 Chili

Mushroom-Beef Stew

Dana R. Moore / Rochester, NY

1 pound beef stew meat
1 can (10¾ ounces) condensed cream of mushroom soup, undiluted
2 cans (4 ounces each) sliced mushrooms, drained
1 package (1 ounce) dry onion soup mix

Combine all ingredients in slow cooker. Cover; cook on LOW 8 to 10 hours.

Makes 4 servings

Dana says: Serve this stew over hot cooked seasoned noodles or rice.

Slow Cooker Veggie Stew

Lin Tuschong / Fort Lauderdale, FL

1 tablespoon vegetable oil
⅔ cup sliced carrots
½ cup diced onion
2 cloves garlic, chopped
2 cans (14 ounces each) fat-free vegetable broth
1½ cups chopped green cabbage
½ cup cut green beans
½ cup diced zucchini
1 tablespoon tomato paste
½ teaspoon dried basil leaves
½ teaspoon dried oregano leaves
¼ teaspoon salt

1. Heat oil in medium skillet over medium-high heat. Add carrots, onion and garlic. Cook and stir until tender.

2. Place carrot mixture and remaining ingredients in slow cooker; stir to combine. Cover; cook on LOW 8 to 10 hours or on HIGH 3 hours.

Makes 4 to 6 servings

Mushroom-Beef Stew

Hamburger Soup

Scarlet Waxman / Orlando, FL

1 pound lean ground beef
1 package (1 ounce) dry onion soup mix
1 package (1 ounce) Italian salad dressing mix
¼ teaspoon seasoned salt
¼ teaspoon black pepper
3 cups boiling water
1 can (8 ounces) diced tomatoes, undrained
1 can (8 ounces) tomato sauce
1 tablespoon soy sauce
1 cup sliced celery
1 cup thinly sliced carrots
2 cups cooked macaroni
¼ cup grated Parmesan cheese
2 tablespoons chopped fresh parsley

1. Brown beef in medium skillet over medium-high heat; drain. Add beef, soup mix, salad dressing mix, seasoned salt and pepper to slow cooker. Add water, tomatoes with juice, tomato sauce and soy sauce; stir to combine. Add celery and carrots. Cover; cook on LOW 6 to 8 hours.

2. *Increase heat to HIGH;* stir in cooked macaroni and Parmesan cheese. Cover; cook 10 to 15 minutes. Sprinkle with parsley just before serving. *Makes 6 to 8 servings*

Tip

Two medium ribs of celery (trimmed of leaves) yield about one cup of chopped celery.

Hamburger Soup

Easy Beef Burgundy

Denise Mayer / Modesto, CA

1½ pounds beef round steak, cut into 1-inch pieces, or beef stew meat
1 can (10¾ ounces) condensed cream of mushroom soup, undiluted
1 cup red wine
1 small onion, chopped
1 can (4 ounces) sliced mushrooms, drained
1 package (1 ounce) dry onion soup mix
1 tablespoon minced garlic

Combine all ingredients in slow cooker. Cover; cook on LOW 6 to 8 hours or until beef is tender. *Makes 4 to 6 servings*

Denise says: Serve this beef over noodles, rice or mashed potatoes. I sometimes also add vegetables for a wonderful stew.

Beef Boogie Woogie

Ruth Ann Haskins / Hoquiam, WA

1 can (10¾ ounces) condensed cream of mushroom soup, undiluted
½ cup chicken broth
1 package (1 ounce) dry onion soup mix
½ teaspoon dried thyme leaves
2 pounds lean beef stew meat
2 cups baby carrots
8 ounces mushrooms, sliced

1. Combine mushroom soup, broth, dry onion soup mix and thyme in slow cooker; mix well.

2. Add remaining ingredients and stir until evenly coated. Cover; cook on HIGH 4 hours or on LOW 8 to 10 hours or until meat is tender.

Makes 8 servings

Ruth Ann says: Serve this dish over noodles or with mashed potatoes. Sprinkle with parsley before serving.

Swiss Steak Stew

Mona Fraser / Kinross, IA

½ cup all-purpose flour, divided
½ teaspoon salt
1½ pounds boneless beef round steak, cut into bite-size pieces
Nonstick cooking spray
3 cups peeled and quartered red potatoes
1 medium onion, diced
1 can (14½ ounces) Italian-style diced tomatoes, undrained
¾ cup water
1 cup canned or frozen corn, thawed

1. Combine ¼ cup flour and salt in large bowl. Add beef; stir to coat.

2. Coat nonstick skillet with cooking spray; heat over medium-low heat. Add beef; brown on all sides.

3. Layer potatoes, beef and onion in slow cooker. Combine tomatoes with juice, water and remaining ¼ cup flour in medium bowl. Pour over ingredients in slow cooker. Cover; cook on LOW 7 to 8 hours or until beef is tender. Add corn; cover and cook on LOW an additional 30 minutes. *Makes 6 servings*

Tip

Follow the manufacturer's instructions for cleaning your slow cooker. To make cleanup even easier, spray the inside of your slow cooker with nonstick cooking spray before adding the recipe ingredients.

Chili with Chocolate

Shawna Steffen / Willmar, MN

- 1 pound lean ground beef
- 1 medium onion, chopped
- 3 cloves garlic, minced, divided
- 1 can (28 ounces) diced tomatoes, undrained
- 1 can (15½ ounces) chili beans in mild or spicy sauce, undrained
- 1½ tablespoons chili powder
- 1 tablespoon grated semisweet baking chocolate
- 1½ teaspoons cumin
- ½ teaspoon salt
- ½ teaspoon black pepper
- ½ teaspoon hot pepper sauce

1. Brown ground beef, onion and 1 clove garlic in large nonstick skillet over medium-low heat, stirring to break up meat; drain fat.

2. Place meat mixture in slow cooker. Add remaining ingredients, including remaining 2 cloves garlic; mix well. Cover; cook on LOW 5 to 6 hours. Garnish as desired.

Makes 4 servings

Tip

The chocolate intensifies the bold and hearty flavor of this chili.

Chili with Chocolate

Clam Chowder

Karen Bassett / Citrus Heights, CA

5 cans (10¾ ounces each) condensed reduced-fat cream of potato soup, undiluted
2 cans (12 ounces each) evaporated skimmed milk
2 cans (10 ounces each) whole baby clams, rinsed and drained
1 can (14¾ ounces) cream-style corn
2 cans (4 ounces each) tiny shrimp, rinsed and drained
¾ cup crisp-cooked and crumbled bacon (about ½ pound) or imitation bacon bits
Lemon pepper to taste
Oyster crackers

Combine all ingredients except crackers in slow cooker. Cover; cook on LOW 3 to 4 hours, stirring occasionally. Serve with oyster crackers.

Makes 10 servings

Easy Beef Stew

Julie Miller-Longo / St. Charles, IL

1½ to 2 pounds beef stew meat
4 medium potatoes, cubed
4 carrots, cut into 1½-inch pieces, *or* 4 cups baby carrots
1 medium onion, cut into 8 pieces
2 cans (8 ounces each) tomato sauce
1 teaspoon salt
½ teaspoon black pepper

Combine all ingredients in slow cooker. Cover; cook on LOW 8 to 10 hours or until vegetables are tender.

Makes 6 to 8 servings

Clam Chowder

Beef Stew

Shannon Lackey / Pineville, NC

1 pound potatoes, cut into 1-inch cubes
1 pound baby carrots
1 large onion, chopped, *or* 1 package (10 ounces) frozen peas and pearl onions
2 pounds beef stew meat
1 can (10¾ ounces) condensed cream of mushroom soup, undiluted
1 can (10¾ ounces) condensed French onion soup, undiluted

Place potatoes in bottom of slow cooker; top with carrots and onion. Add stew meat. Pour soups over top. Cover; cook on LOW 8 to 10 hours. *Makes 8 servings*

Chicken Stew

Terri Murr / Roanoke, AL

4 to 5 cups chopped cooked chicken
1 can (28 ounces) whole tomatoes, undrained
2 large potatoes, cut into 1-inch pieces
½ pound okra, sliced
1 large onion, chopped
1 can (14 ounces) cream-style corn
½ cup ketchup
½ cup barbecue sauce

1. Combine chicken, tomatoes with juice, potatoes, okra and onion in slow cooker. Cover; cook on LOW 6 to 8 hours or until potatoes are tender.

2. Add corn, ketchup and barbecue sauce. Cover; cook on HIGH 30 minutes. *Makes 6 servings*

Terri says: Serve this stew with hot crusty rolls and a green salad, and your meal is complete.

Ranch Stew

Ramona Hook Wysong / Barlow, KY

2 pounds beef stew meat
6 medium potatoes, diced
2 cups sliced carrots
2 medium onions, chopped
1 medium green bell pepper, chopped (optional)
1 cup diced celery (optional)
1 can (10¾ ounces) condensed tomato soup, undiluted
1 soup can water
2 tablespoons tapioca
1 tablespoon Worcestershire sauce
2 teaspoons salt
1 teaspoon soy sauce
¼ teaspoon black pepper
1 bay leaf

Combine all ingredients in slow cooker. Cover; cook on LOW 10 to 12 hours or until meat and vegetables are tender. Remove and discard bay leaf before serving. *Makes 6 servings*

Veggie Soup with Beef

Wanda Fortenberry / Elizabeth City, NC

1 pound beef stew meat
2 cans (15 ounces each) mixed vegetables
1 can (8 ounces) tomato sauce
2 cloves garlic, minced
Water

Place all ingredients in slow cooker. Add enough water to fill slow cooker to within ½ inch of top. Cover; cook on LOW 8 to 10 hours.

Makes 4 servings

sandwich **selection**

BBQ Beef Sandwiches

Susan Revely / Ashland, KY

1 boneless beef chuck roast (about 3 pounds)
¼ cup ketchup
2 tablespoons brown sugar
2 tablespoons red wine vinegar
1 tablespoon Dijon mustard
1 tablespoon Worcestershire sauce
1 clove garlic, crushed
¼ teaspoon salt
¼ teaspoon liquid smoke
⅛ teaspoon black pepper
10 to 12 French rolls or sandwich buns

1. Place beef in slow cooker. Combine remaining ingredients except rolls in medium bowl; pour over meat in slow cooker. Cover; cook on LOW 8 to 9 hours.

2. Remove beef from slow cooker; shred with 2 forks. Combine beef with 1 cup sauce from slow cooker. Spoon mixture onto warmed rolls. Top with additional sauce, if desired. *Makes 10 to 12 servings*

Susan says: This recipe keeps beautifully in the fridge once it is cooked. Just reheat it in the microwave or on your stove top.

BBQ Beef Sandwich

Spicy Shredded Chicken

Amanda Neelley / Spring Hill, TN

6 boneless skinless chicken breasts (about 1½ pounds)
1 jar (16 ounces) salsa

Place chicken in slow cooker. Cover with salsa. Cover; cook on LOW 6 to 8 hours. Shred chicken with two forks before serving.

Makes 6 servings

Amanda says: Serve on warm flour tortillas with taco fixings.

Roast Beef Burritos

Tori Herrera / Silverdale, WA

1 boneless beef rump or bottom round roast (3 to 5 pounds)
¼ cup water
Garlic powder
Black pepper
1 bay leaf
2 jars (16 ounces each) salsa
2 cans (4 ounces each) diced green chilies, undrained
½ large yellow onion, diced

1. Place roast in slow cooker; add water. Season with garlic powder and pepper to taste. Add bay leaf. Cover; cook on HIGH 6 hours or until meat is tender. Remove and discard bay leaf.

2. Removed meat to cutting board. Trim and discard fat. Shred meat, using 2 forks.

3. Skim fat from liquid in slow cooker. Add shredded beef, salsa, chilies and onion to liquid; stir to combine. Cover; cook on HIGH 1 hour or until onion is tender.

Makes 8 to 10 servings

Tori says: Scoop about 3 tablespoons of meat onto a burrito-size flour tortilla. Top with cheese, and fold into a burrito. Place seam-side-down on a plate. Microwave for 30 seconds to melt the cheese. Serve the burrito with refried beans and Mexican rice. This also works great for cooked roast leftovers.

Spicy Shredded Chicken

Easy Beefy Sandwiches

Kristen Grotewiel / St. Charles, MO

1 boneless beef rump roast (2 to 4 pounds)
1 package (1 ounce) Italian salad dressing mix
1 package (1 ounce) dry onion soup mix
2 cubes beef bouillon
2 tablespoons prepared yellow mustard
Garlic powder
Onion powder
Salt
Black pepper
1 cup water

Place roast, salad dressing mix, soup mix, bouillon cubes and mustard in slow cooker. Season to taste with garlic powder, onion powder, salt and pepper. Add water. Cover; cook on LOW 8 to 10 hours.

Makes 6 to 8 servings

Kristen says: Slice the roast and serve it with provolone, mozzarella or Lorraine Swiss cheese on hard rolls.

Tip

Keep a lid on it! A slow cooker can take as long as 20 minutes to regain the heat lost when the cover is removed. If a recipe calls for stirring or checking the dish near the end of the cooking time, replace the lid as quickly as possible.

Easy Beefy Sandwich

Easy Family Burritos

Priss Lindsey / Albuquerque, NM

1 beef roast (2 to 3 pounds)
1 jar (24 ounces) *or* 2 jars (16 ounces each) salsa
Flour tortillas

1. Place roast in slow cooker; top with salsa. Cover; cook on LOW 8 to 10 hours.

2. Remove meat from slow cooker. Shred with 2 forks. Return to slow cooker; cook 1 to 2 hours more. Serve shredded meat wrapped in tortillas. *Makes 8 servings*

Priss says: Garnish your burritos with any combination of the following: shredded cheese, sour cream, salsa, lettuce, tomato, onion and guacamole. I sometimes make a batch of burrito meat and freeze it in family-size portions. It's quick and easy to reheat in the microwave on busy nights when there is no time to cook.

Italian Beef

Ramona Hook Wysong / Barlow, KY

1 boneless beef chuck shoulder roast (5 to 6 pounds), cut in half
3½ cups water
4 medium green bell peppers, sliced
1 onion, sliced
3 tablespoons vinegar
3 teaspoons caraway seeds
1½ teaspoons salt
½ teaspoon black pepper
¼ teaspoon dried oregano leaves
3 bay leaves

Combine all ingredients in slow cooker. Cover; cook on LOW 8 to 12 hours or until very tender. Remove and discard bay leaves before serving. *Makes 8 to 10 servings*

Ramona says: We love to shred the meat with forks, and then serve it on buns.

Easy Family Burritos

Easy Homemade Barbecue

Dawn Sunkle / West Columbia, SC

Water
1 boneless pork blade (butt) roast (3 to 4 pounds)
Salt
Black pepper
1 bottle (16 ounces) barbecue sauce
Hamburger buns or sandwich rolls

1. Cover bottom of slow cooker with water. Place roast in slow cooker; season with salt and pepper to taste. Cover; cook on LOW 8 to 10 hours.

2. Remove roast from slow cooker; let stand 15 minutes. Discard liquid remaining in slow cooker. Using 2 forks, shred cooked roast. Return meat to slow cooker. Add barbecue sauce; mix well. Cover; cook on HIGH 30 minutes. To serve, spoon barbecue mixture onto buns.

Makes 8 to 10 servings

Dawn says: Depending on the size of your roast, you may not need to use an entire bottle of barbecue sauce. This recipe is equally tasty when made with other cuts of pork roast.

Tip

These delicious barbecue sandwiches are always sure to please—whether served at super-bowl parties, potluck dinners, or simple weeknight meals.

Easy Homemade Barbecue

Roast Beef Po' Boys

Heather Deville / Baker, LA

1 boneless beef chuck shoulder roast (4 to 5 pounds), cut into cubes
Cajun seasoning or seasoned salt
¼ cup cornstarch
½ cup water
Few drops liquid gravy browner (optional)
French bread, sliced

1. Coat meat with Cajun seasoning to taste; place in slow cooker. Cover; cook on HIGH 4 hours or until tender.

2. Remove meat to cutting board; allow to cool slightly. Trim and discard fat from beef. Shred meat, using 2 forks.

3. Skim fat from surface of liquid in slow cooker. Dissolve cornstarch in water in small bowl. Add to slow cooker, along with liquid gravy browner, if desired; mix well. Cook on LOW 15 minutes or until liquid is thickened.

4. Return shredded meat to slow cooker; stir well. Cover; cook at least 30 minutes or until warm. Serve over sliced bread.

Makes 10 servings

Savory Italian Beef

Karen Wise / Springfield, IL

1 beef chuck shoulder roast (3 to 4 pounds)
2 packages (1 ounce each) Italian salad dressing mix
1 package (1 ounce) dry onion soup mix
1 can (12 ounces) beer or beef broth
1 tablespoon cornstarch (optional)
2 tablespoons water (optional)

1. Place roast in slow cooker; sprinkle salad dressing mix and soup mix over meat. Pour beer over top. Cover; cook on LOW 8 to 10 hours.

2. Remove meat from slow cooker; allow to cool slightly. Shred meat, using 2 forks.

3. Skim fat from surface of liquid in slow cooker. For thicker gravy, if desired, stir cornstarch into water in small bowl until no longer lumpy. Add cornstarch mixture to liquid in slow cooker; mix well. Cook on HIGH 15 minutes or until thickened.

4. Return shredded meat to slow cooker. Cover; cook on HIGH 15 to 30 minutes or until warm. *Makes 6 servings*

Karen says: If using a dense roast such as rump or sirloin tip, make 2 or 3 deep cuts through the meat, so seasonings are evenly distributed. Serve cooked beef on sandwich buns or over mashed potatoes.

Super-Easy Beef Burritos

Ronell Sheafer / Calimesa, CA

1 boneless beef roast (2 to 3 pounds)
1 can (28 ounces) enchilada sauce
Water (optional)
4 (8-inch) flour tortillas

Place roast in slow cooker; cover with enchilada sauce. Add a little water, if desired. Cover and cook on LOW 6 to 8 hours or until beef begins to fall apart. Serve cooked beef in tortillas. Garnish as desired.

Makes 4 servings

Ronell says: Our favorite garnishes include shredded cheese, sour cream, salsa, lettuce and tomatoes.

Italian Combo Subs

Valorie Rowland / Hardin, KY

1 tablespoon vegetable oil
1 pound boneless beef round steak, cut into thin strips
1 pound Italian sausage
1 green bell pepper, cut into strips
1 medium onion, thinly sliced
1 can (4 ounces) sliced mushrooms, drained (optional)
Salt
Black pepper
1 jar (26 ounces) spaghetti sauce
2 loaves Italian bread, cut into 1-inch-thick slices

1. Heat oil in large skillet over medium-high heat. Gently brown steak strips; drain fat. Place steak in slow cooker.

2. Brown Italian sausage in same skillet until no longer pink; drain fat. Add sausage to slow cooker.

3. Place bell pepper, onion and mushrooms, if desired, over meat in slow cooker. Season with salt and black pepper to taste. Top with spaghetti sauce. Cover; cook on LOW 4 to 6 hours. Serve mixture on bread.

Makes 6 servings

Tip

Try these subs topped with freshly grated Parmesan cheese.

Italian Combo Sub

Spicy Italian Beef

Barbara Mohrle / Dallas, TX

1 boneless beef chuck roast (3 to 4 pounds)
1 jar (12 ounces) peperoncini (mild salad peppers)
1 can (14½ ounces) beef broth
1 can (12 ounces) beer
1 package (1 ounce) Italian salad dressing mix
1 loaf French bread, thickly sliced
10 slices provolone cheese (optional)

1. Trim visible fat from roast. Cut roast, if necessary, to fit in slow cooker, leaving meat in as many large pieces as possible.

2. Drain peppers; pull off stem ends and discard. Add peppers, broth, beer and salad dressing mix to slow cooker; *do not stir*. Cover; cook on LOW 8 to 10 hours.

3. Remove meat from slow cooker; shred with 2 forks. Return shredded meat to slow cooker; mix well. Serve on French bread slice, topped with cheese, if desired. Add additional sauce and peppers as desired.

Makes 8 to 10 servings

Tip

Peperoncini are pickled Tuscan peppers. These peppers taste mildly sweet and range in heat from medium to medium-hot.

Spicy Italian Beef

Easy Beef Sandwiches

Tosha Romanoff / Union Bridge, MD

1 large onion, sliced
1 boneless beef bottom round roast (3 to 5 pounds)
1 cup water
1 package (1 ounce) au jus gravy mix

Place onion slices in bottom of slow cooker; top with roast. Combine water and au jus mix in small bowl; pour over roast. Cover; cook on LOW 7 to 9 hours. *Makes 6 to 8 servings*

Tosha says: Before serving, shred the meat in the slow cooker. Serve it on French bread, with the liquid from the slow cooker on the side. Try it topped with provolone cheese for a fantastic sandwich.

Tavern Burger

Diane Lindner / Fanwood, NJ

2 pounds extra-lean ground beef
½ cup ketchup
¼ cup brown sugar
¼ cup prepared yellow mustard
Hamburger buns

1. Brown beef in medium skillet over medium-high heat, stirring frequently to break up meat; drain fat.

2. Place beef and remaining ingredients in slow cooker; mix well. Cover; cook on LOW 4 to 6 hours. Serve on buns. *Makes 8 servings*

Diane says: Serve a scoopful on a hamburger bun. This is also known to some people as "BBQ's" or "loose-meat sandwiches." I usually don't measure ingredients for this; I just go by taste. For added flavor, add a can of pork and beans.

Easy Beef Sandwich

noodles & **rice**

Chinese Cashew Chicken

Barb Gartzke / Sullivan, WI

1 pound bean sprouts (fresh or canned)
2 cups sliced cooked chicken
1 can (10¾ ounces) condensed cream of mushroom soup, undiluted
1 cup sliced celery
½ cup chopped green onion
1 can (4 ounces) sliced mushrooms, drained
3 tablespoons butter
1 tablespoon soy sauce
1 cup cashews

Combine all ingredients except cashews in slow cooker. Cover; cook on LOW 4 to 6 hours or on HIGH 3 to 4 hours. Just before serving, stir in cashews. *Makes 4 servings*

Barb says: Serve with rice or noodles.

Tip

This dish is a perfect way to make use of leftover chicken.

Chinese Cashew Chicken

Easy Beef Stroganoff

Mary Braam / Raleigh, NC

3 cans (10¾ ounces each) condensed cream of chicken or cream of mushroom soup, undiluted
1 cup sour cream
½ cup water
1 package (1 ounce) dry onion soup mix
2 pounds beef stew meat

Combine soup, sour cream, water and dry onion soup mix in slow cooker. Add beef; stir until well coated. Cover; cook on HIGH 3 hours or on LOW 6 hours. *Makes 4 to 6 servings*

Mary says: Serve this beef over rice or noodles, along with a salad and hot bread. You can reduce the calories and fat in this dish by using 98% fat-free soup and fat-free sour cream.

Nicole's Favorite Slow Cooker Chicken Cacciatore

Jane Paquet / Unionville, CT

6 boneless skinless chicken breasts (about 1½ pounds)
Garlic powder
Onion powder
Seasoned salt
Italian seasoning
Black pepper
10 ounces mushrooms, sliced
1 can (15 ounces) Italian-style tomato sauce
¼ cup red wine or chicken broth
8 ounces bow-tie pasta, cooked according to package directions

1. Spray inside of slow cooker with nonstick cooking spray. Place chicken in slow cooker. Sprinkle generously with seasonings to taste.

2. Add mushrooms. Pour tomato sauce and wine over top. Cover; cook on LOW 6 hours. Serve with hot cooked pasta. *Makes 6 servings*

Jane says: I sometimes use frozen boneless skinless chicken breasts and increase the cooking time to 8 hours on LOW.

Easy Beef Stroganoff

Slow Cooker Stuffed Peppers

Susan Ambrose / Cabot, PA

1 package (about 7 ounces) Spanish rice mix
1 pound ground beef
½ cup diced celery
1 small onion, chopped
1 egg
4 medium green bell peppers, halved lengthwise, cored and seeded
1 can (28 ounces) whole peeled tomatoes, undrained
1 can (10¾ ounces) condensed tomato soup, undiluted
1 cup water

1. Set aside seasoning packet from rice. Combine beef, rice mix, celery, onion and egg in large bowl. Divide meat mixture evenly among pepper halves.

2. Pour tomatoes with juice into slow cooker. Arrange filled pepper halves on top of tomatoes. Combine tomato soup, water and reserved rice mix seasoning packet in medium bowl. Pour over peppers. Cover; cook on LOW 8 to 10 hours. *Makes 4 servings*

Beef and Noodles

Karen Kreuzer / Pittsburgh, PA

1 tablespoon vegetable oil
1 beef chuck shoulder roast (3 pounds)
1 can (10¾ ounces) condensed cream of mushroom or cream of potato soup, undiluted
1 cup cooking sherry
1 cup water
1 package (1 ounce) dry onion soup mix
1 package (12 ounces) egg noodles, cooked according to package directions

1. Heat oil in large skillet over medium-low heat. Brown roast on all sides; drain fat.

2. Place meat and remaining ingredients except noodles in slow cooker. Cover; cook on LOW 8 hours, stirring once or twice during cooking. Serve roast over hot cooked noodles. *Makes 8 servings*

Slow Cooker Stuffed Peppers

Slow Cooker Chicken & Rice

Tami Stapleton / Darlington, SC

3 cans (10¾ ounces each) condensed cream of chicken soup, undiluted
2 cups instant rice, uncooked
1 cup water
1 pound boneless skinless chicken breasts or chicken breast tenders
½ teaspoon salt
¼ teaspoon black pepper
¼ teaspoon paprika
½ cup diced celery

Combine soup, rice and water in slow cooker. Add chicken; sprinkle with salt, pepper and paprika. Sprinkle celery over top of chicken. Cover; cook on HIGH 3 to 4 hours or on LOW 6 to 8 hours.

Makes 4 servings

Chicken Azteca

Pam Fierro / Virginia Beach, VA

2 cups frozen corn
1 can (15 ounces) black beans, rinsed and drained
1 cup chunky salsa, divided
1 clove garlic, minced
½ teaspoon ground cumin
4 boneless skinless chicken breasts (about 1 pound)
1 package (8 ounces) cream cheese, cubed
Hot cooked rice
Shredded Cheddar cheese

1. Combine corn, beans, ½ cup salsa, garlic and cumin in slow cooker. Arrange chicken breasts over top; pour remaining ½ cup salsa over chicken. Cover; cook on HIGH 2 to 3 hours or on LOW 4 to 6 hours or until chicken is tender.

2. Remove chicken; cut into bite-size pieces. Return chicken to slow cooker. Add cream cheese. Cook on HIGH until cream cheese melts and blends into sauce. Spoon chicken and sauce over rice. Top with Cheddar cheese.

Makes 4 servings

Slow Cooker Chicken & Rice

Red Beans and Rice with Ham

Cheryl Hulbert / Newnan, GA

1 package (16 ounces) dried red beans
1 pound beef smoked sausage, sliced
1 ham slice (about 8 ounces), cubed
1 small onion, diced
2½ to 3 cups water
⅛ teaspoon ground red pepper
1 teaspoon Mexican (adobo) seasoning with pepper
Hot cooked white rice

1. Soak beans overnight; rinse and drain.

2. Place beans in slow cooker. Add sausage, ham, onion and water (3 cups for HIGH; 2½ cups for LOW). Season with red pepper and Mexican seasoning. Cover; cook on HIGH 3 to 4 hours or on LOW 7 to 8 hours or until beans are tender, stirring every 2 hours if necessary. Serve over rice. *Makes 6 servings*

Heather's Chicken Tetrazzini

Heather Moore / Jacksons Gap, AL

4 to 6 boneless skinless chicken breasts (about 1 to 1½ pounds)
Garlic salt
Lemon-pepper seasoning
1 can (10¾ ounces) condensed cream of chicken soup, undiluted
1 can (10¾ ounces) condensed cream of broccoli soup, undiluted
1 package (16 ounces) spaghetti
Grated Parmesan cheese (optional)

1. Place chicken in slow cooker; sprinkle with garlic salt and lemon-pepper seasoning to taste. Pour soups over top. Cover; cook on LOW 6 to 8 hours.

2. Before serving, cook spaghetti according to package directions; drain. Serve chicken over spaghetti. Sprinkle with grated Parmesan cheese, if desired. *Makes 4 to 6 servings*

Red Beans and Rice with Ham

Excellent Tailgating Beef & Noodles

Suzi Kuegel / Owensboro, KY

1 beef round steak (2 pounds), cubed
2 jars (10 ounces each) beef gravy
1 package (12 ounces) egg noodles, cooked according to package directions

Place steak in slow cooker; cover with gravy. Cover; cook on LOW 8 to 10 hours. To serve, spoon steak and gravy over hot cooked noodles.

Makes 4 to 6 servings

Suzi says: This is so good. Served with a tossed salad, it makes a great, easy meal.

Favorite Brand Name™

ALL-NEW SLOW COOKER RECIPES

Contents

beef entrées

Suzie's Sloppy Joes

Makes 8 to 10 servings

3 pounds 90% lean ground beef
1 cup chopped onion
3 cloves garlic, minced
1¼ cups ketchup
1 cup chopped red bell pepper
5 tablespoons Worcestershire sauce
¼ cup brown sugar
3 tablespoons vinegar
3 tablespoons prepared mustard
2 teaspoons chili powder
Hamburger buns

1. Cook and stir ground beef, onion and garlic in large skillet over medium-high heat until beef is browned and onion is tender. Drain fat.

2. Combine ketchup, bell pepper, Worcestershire sauce, brown sugar, vinegar, mustard and chili powder in slow cooker. Stir in beef mixture. Cover; cook on LOW 6 to 8 hours. Spoon into hamburger buns.

Suzie's Sloppy Joes

Special Sauerbraten

Makes 6 to 8 servings

2 cups *each* dry red wine and red wine vinegar
2 cups water
2 large onions, sliced
2 large carrots, sliced
¼ cup sugar
1 tablespoon dried parsley flakes
2 teaspoons salt
4 bay leaves
1 teaspoon mustard seed
6 peppercorns
6 whole cloves
4 juniper berries*
1 beef round tip roast (about 5 pounds)
4 tablespoons all-purpose flour, divided
1 teaspoon salt
¼ teaspoon black pepper
2 tablespoons oil
2 tablespoons sugar
⅓ cup gingersnap crumbs

**Juniper berries are available in the spice aisle at large supermarkets or from mail order spice purveyors.*

1. Stir together wine, vinegar, water, onions, carrots, sugar, parsley, salt, bay leaves, mustard seed, peppercorns, cloves and juniper berries in medium saucepan over high heat. Bring to a boil; reduce heat to medium-low and simmer 15 minutes. Cool completely. Place roast in large glass bowl or large resealable plastic food storage bag; pour mixture over roast. Cover or seal bag. Marinate in refrigerator up to 2 days, turning once a day.

2. Remove meat from marinade. Strain marinade, reserving juices. Dry meat with paper towel. Combine 2 tablespoons flour, salt and pepper in small bowl. Coat all sides of meat in flour mixture. Heat oil in large skillet over medium heat. Add meat; brown on all sides.

3. Place meat in slow cooker. Add 1½ cups strained marinade juices. (Discard any remaining marinade.) Cover; cook on LOW 8 hours.

4. Combine sugar, remaining 2 tablespoons flour and gingersnap crumbs in small bowl; add to slow cooker. Stir well. Cover; cook on HIGH 30 minutes.

Note: Sauerbraten is a German dish traditionally marinated 3 or 4 days.

*Favorite recipe from **Linda Lee Chase, Riverhead, NY***

Special Sauerbraten

Slow Cooker Bean Dish

Makes 8 servings

1 pound 95% lean ground beef
½ pound bacon, cut into 1-inch pieces
1 can (15 ounces) butter beans, drained
1 can (15 ounces) garbanzo beans, drained
1 can (15 ounces) red kidney beans, drained
1 can (15 ounces) pork and beans
1 cup brown sugar
1 cup ketchup
½ cup diced onion
2 tablespoons vinegar

1. Cook and stir ground beef in large skillet over medium-high heat until no longer pink. Drain excess fat.

2. Combine beef and remaining ingredients in slow cooker. Cover; cook on LOW 6 hours.

Favorite recipe from ***Wendi Meisenheimer, Baldwin City, KS***

Shredded Beef Chili

Makes 6 to 8 servings

1 beef chuck shoulder roast (2 to 3 pounds)
1 can (15 ounces) corn, drained
1 can (4 ounces) diced green chilies
1 medium onion, diced
2 medium potatoes, diced
Chili powder

1. Place roast, corn and chilies in slow cooker. Cover; cook on LOW 8 to 10 hours.

2. An hour before serving, remove roast and shred with 2 forks. Return meat to slow cooker. Add onion, potatoes and chili powder to taste. Cover; cook on HIGH 1 hour or until potatoes are tender.

Susan says: Top with Colby or Mexican cheese blend and serve either on flour tortillas or over rice. Serve refried beans, lettuce and tomato on the side, if desired.

Favorite recipe from ***Susan Hackitt, Tuscon, AZ***

Paul's Slow Cooker Roast Beef Dinner

Makes 12 servings

1 beef roast (about 3 pounds)
1 tablespoon freshly grated horseradish
1 tablespoon Dijon mustard
1 tablespoon minced fresh parsley
1 teaspoon dried thyme, basil or oregano leaves
1 to 2 pounds Yukon Gold potatoes, peeled and quartered
1 pound mushrooms, cut into large chunks
2 cans (10½ ounces each) beef consommé
2 large tomatoes, seeded and diced
1 large onion, sliced
1 green bell pepper, chopped
1 red bell pepper, chopped
1 cup red wine
3 cloves garlic, minced
1 bay leaf
Salt
Black pepper

1. Place roast in slow cooker. Combine horseradish, Dijon mustard, parsley and thyme in small bowl; spread paste over roast.

2. Add remaining ingredients to slow cooker; season to taste with salt and black pepper. Add enough water to cover roast and vegetables.

3. Cover; cook on HIGH 2 hours. Reduce heat to LOW; cook 4 to 6 hours or until roast and vegetables are tender.

Paul says: The roast drippings can be used for an au jus or gravy. I like to serve this dinner with oven-warmed bread and seasoned butter. A salad and a merlot wine are great complements, too.

Favorite recipe from ***Paul Lance, Bloomington, MN***

Slow Cooker Pepper Steak

Makes 6 to 8 servings

- **2 tablespoons vegetable oil**
- **3 pounds boneless beef top sirloin steak, cut into strips**
- **1 tablespoon minced garlic (5 to 6 cloves)**
- **1 medium onion, chopped**
- **½ cup reduced-sodium soy sauce**
- **2 teaspoons sugar**
- **1 teaspoon salt**
- **½ teaspoon ground ginger**
- **½ teaspoon black pepper**
- **3 green bell peppers, cut into strips**
- **¼ cup cold water**
- **1 tablespoon cornstarch**
- **Hot cooked white rice**

1. Heat oil in large skillet over medium-low heat. Brown steak strips. Add garlic; cook and stir 2 minutes. Transfer steak strips, garlic and pan juices to slow cooker.

2. Add onion, soy sauce, sugar, salt, ginger and black pepper to slow cooker; mix well. Cover; cook on LOW 6 to 8 hours or until meat is tender (up to 10 hours).

3. Add bell pepper strips during final hour of cooking. Before serving, combine water and cornstarch in small bowl; stir into juices in slow cooker. Cook on HIGH 10 minutes or until thickened. Serve with rice.

Favorite recipe from ***Carol Wright, Cartersville, GA***

Slow Cooker Beef Stroganoff

Makes 4 to 6 servings

- **1½ to 2 pounds beef for stew**
- **1 can (10¾ ounces) condensed cream of mushroom soup, undiluted**
- **1 can (4 ounces) sliced mushrooms, drained**
- **1 package (1 ounce) dry onion soup mix**
- **Hot cooked noodles or rice**

Combine beef, mushroom soup, mushrooms and onion soup mix in slow cooker. Cover; cook on LOW 6 to 8 hours.

Irene says: Serve this beef with hot cooked rice or noodles.

Favorite recipe from ***Irene Thomas, Owatonna, MN***

Slow Cooker Pepper Steak

Cocktail Meatballs

Makes 12 servings

1 pound ground beef
1 pound bulk pork sausage or Italian sausage
1 cup cracker crumbs
1 cup finely chopped onion
1 cup finely chopped green bell pepper
½ cup milk
1 egg, beaten
2 teaspoons salt
1 teaspoon dried Italian seasoning
¼ teaspoon black pepper
1 cup ketchup
¾ cup brown sugar
½ cup (1 stick) margarine or butter
½ cup vinegar
¼ cup lemon juice
¼ cup water
1 teaspoon prepared mustard
¼ teaspoon garlic salt

1. Preheat oven to 350°F. Combine beef, sausage, cracker crumbs, onion, bell pepper, milk, egg, salt, Italian seasoning and black pepper in large bowl; mix well. Form into 1-inch meatballs. Place meatballs on nonstick baking sheets. Bake 25 minutes or until browned.

2. Meanwhile, add ketchup, sugar, margarine, vinegar, lemon juice, water, mustard and garlic salt to slow cooker; mix well. Cover; cook on HIGH until hot.

3. Transfer meatballs to slow cooker; carefully stir to coat with sauce. Reduce heat to LOW. Cover; cook 2 hours.

Billie says: Serve on toothpicks or insert pretzel sticks to let guests help themselves.

Favorite recipe from ***Billie Olofson, Des Moines, IA***

Barbecue Beef Cubes

Makes 8 servings

1 boneless beef chuck shoulder roast (about 4 pounds), cut into cubes
1 can (28 ounces) diced or stewed tomatoes, undrained
1 can (4 ounces) tomato paste
1 large onion, chopped
¼ cup firmly packed brown sugar
¼ cup vinegar
2 teaspoons salt
2 teaspoons barbecue spice mix
2 teaspoons Worcestershire sauce
2 cloves garlic, minced
1 teaspoon dry mustard
¼ teaspoon black pepper

Place beef cubes in slow cooker. Combine remaining ingredients in large bowl; pour over meat. Cover; cook on LOW 6 to 8 hours or until tender.

Beth says: Serve over rice or noodles. This recipe also works great with spareribs, instead of roast.

Favorite recipe from ***Beth Colwell, Willow Street, PA***

St. Patrick's Day Dinner

Makes 16 to 18 servings

6 potatoes, peeled and halved
1 pound peeled baby carrots
4 pounds corned beef brisket, trimmed of all visible fat
3 cloves garlic, minced
6 medium yellow onions, cut into thick wedges
1 medium head cabbage, cleaned and cut into 6 wedges

1. Place potatoes and carrots in slow cooker; add enough water to cover.

2. Place beef in slow cooker over vegetables. Sprinkle with garlic; top with onions. Cover; cook on LOW 10 hours (or on HIGH 1 hour and on LOW 7 hours). Add cabbage wedges to top of slow cooker during last 2 hours of cooking, or steam separately and drizzle with drippings from bottom of slow cooker.

Cathie says: Every year my family and friends look forward to my annual St. Patrick's Day Dinner. This recipe requires a 6-quart slow cooker.

Favorite recipe from ***Cathie Rausch, Palatine, IL***

Cabbage Rolls

Makes 16 servings

1 large head cabbage, cored
Salt
3 pounds ground beef
1 pound pork sausage
2 medium onions, chopped
1½ cups cooked rice
1 egg
2 tablespoons prepared horseradish
2 tablespoons ketchup
1 package (1 ounce) dry onion soup mix
1 tablespoon salt
1 teaspoon allspice
½ teaspoon garlic powder
Black pepper
Sauce for Cabbage Rolls (page 135)

1. Place cabbage, core-side down, in large stockpot filled halfway with salted water. Simmer over medium heat 5 minutes or until outside leaves come off easily. Continue to simmer and pull out rest of leaves. Set leaves aside; reserve water.

2. Stir together remaining ingredients except Sauce for Cabbage Rolls in large bowl. Roll meat mixture into 3-inch balls. Place 1 meatball on cabbage leaf. Roll up leaf. Fold in edges and secure with toothpick. Repeat with remaining meatballs and cabbage leaves.

3. Place cabbage rolls in slow cooker. Cover; cook on LOW 5 hours. Serve sauce over tops of rolls.

Shirley says: I came up with this recipe years ago. One of my children didn't like tomatoes, so I omitted them from the sauce and used cheese soup, instead. Through the years, I have added more spices. If you don't like cheese, you could make the sauce with stewed tomatoes and tomato sauce, instead. We have this when I have eight extra people for dinner—and we still have enough for the next day!

Favorite recipe from ***Shirley McLear, Manistique, MI***

Cabbage Rolls

Garden Swiss Steak

Makes 12 to 14 servings

- **½ cup all-purpose flour**
- **2 teaspoons seasoned salt**
- **1 teaspoon black pepper**
- **2 tablespoons olive oil**
- **3 to 4 pounds boneless beef round steak, trimmed of all visible fat**
- **3 cans (14½ ounces each) diced or stewed tomatoes**
- **3 large green bell peppers, seeded and cut into ¾-inch strips**
- **2 large onions, cut into ½-inch wedges**
- **¼ cup steak sauce**
- **Hot cooked white rice**

1. Combine flour, seasoned salt and black pepper in shallow bowl.

2. Cut beef into 4- to 6-ounce servings. Dredge in seasoned flour. Reserve leftover flour. Heat oil in medium skillet over medium-high heat until hot. Add beef; brown both sides. Set aside.

3. Transfer reserved flour to small bowl. Slowly add water, stirring with fork, to make thin paste.

4. Place beef in slow cooker; add flour paste, tomatoes, bell peppers, onions and steak sauce.

5. Cover; cook on LOW 10 to 12 hours. Serve over rice.

Cathie says: This is a great recipe to fix when your garden is producing faster than you can use the vegetables.

Favorite recipe from ***Cathie Rausch, Palatine, IL***

Fantastic Pot Roast

Makes 6 servings

- **1 boneless beef chuck roast (about 2½ pounds)**
- **1 can (12 ounces) cola**
- **1 bottle (10 ounces) chili sauce**
- **2 cloves garlic (optional)**

Combine all ingredients in slow cooker. Cover; cook on HIGH 5 hours.

Favorite recipe from ***Patricia Campbell Molle, Pompano Beach, FL***

Slow-Cooked Pot Roast

Makes 6 to 8 servings

1 tablespoon vegetable oil
1 beef brisket (3 to 4 pounds)
1 tablespoon garlic powder, divided
1 tablespoon salt, divided
1 tablespoon black pepper, divided
1 teaspoon paprika, divided
5 to 6 new potatoes, cut into quarters
4 to 5 medium onions, sliced
1 pound baby carrots
1 can (14½ ounces) beef broth

1. Heat 1 tablespoon oil on HIGH in slow cooker. Brown brisket on all sides. Remove brisket to plate. Season with 1½ teaspoons garlic powder, 1½ teaspoons salt, 1½ teaspoons pepper and ½ teaspoon paprika; set aside.

2. Season potatoes with remaining 1½ teaspoons garlic powder, 1½ teaspoons salt, 1½ teaspoons pepper and ½ teaspoon paprika. Add potatoes and onions to slow cooker. Cook on HIGH, stirring occasionally, until browned.

3. Return brisket to slow cooker over potatoes and onions. Add carrots and broth. Cover; cook on HIGH 4 to 5 hours or on LOW 8 to 10 hours or until meat is tender.

Marsha says: To serve, arrange the potatoes and carrots around the sliced beef. Spoon on broth to keep the meat moist.

Favorite recipe from ***Marsha Kimmelman, East Meadow, NY***

That's Italian Meat Loaf

Makes 8 servings

1 can (8 ounces) tomato sauce, divided
1 egg, lightly beaten
½ cup chopped onion
½ cup chopped green bell pepper
⅓ cup dry seasoned bread crumbs
2 tablespoons grated Parmesan cheese
½ teaspoon garlic powder
¼ teaspoon black pepper
1 pound ground beef
½ pound ground pork or veal
1 cup shredded Asiago cheese

1. Reserve ⅓ cup tomato sauce; set aside in refrigerator. Combine remaining tomato sauce and egg in large bowl. Add onion, bell pepper, bread crumbs, Parmesan cheese, garlic powder and black pepper; mix well. Add ground beef and pork; mix well and shape into loaf.

2. Place meat loaf on foil strips. Place in slow cooker. Cover; cook on LOW 8 to 10 hours or on HIGH 4 to 6 hours or until internal temperature reaches 170°F when tested with a meat thermometer inserted into thickest part of meat loaf.

3. Spread meat loaf with reserved ⅓ cup tomato sauce. Sprinkle with Asiago cheese. Cover and cook 15 minutes or until cheese is melted. Using foil strips, remove meat loaf from slow cooker.

BBQ Roast Beef

Makes 10 to 12 sandwiches

2 pounds boneless cooked roast beef
1 bottle (12 ounces) barbecue sauce
1½ cups water
Sandwich rolls

Combine all ingredients in slow cooker. Cover; cook on LOW 2 hours. Shred with 2 forks. Serve on sandwich rolls.

Favorite recipe from ***Debra Tatta, Sharpsville, PA***

That's Italian Meat Loaf

Saucy Braised Beef

Makes 4 to 6 servings

1 boneless beef round steak (about 2 pounds), trimmed and cut into bite-size pieces
1 tablespoon mixed dried herbs
Salt
Black pepper
2 tablespoons vegetable oil
2 cups baby carrots
1 large yellow onion, thinly sliced
1 medium zucchini, cut into 1-inch slices
2 tablespoons minced garlic
1 teaspoon dried oregano leaves
1 can (8 ounces) tomato sauce
1 can (6 ounces) tomato paste
½ cup dark molasses
2 tablespoons red wine vinegar
2 teaspoons hot pepper sauce
Hot cooked noodles

1. Lightly season beef with mixed herbs, salt and pepper to taste. Heat oil in Dutch oven or large skillet over medium-low heat. Brown meat on all sides. Drain fat; discard. Place beef in slow cooker.

2. Add carrots, onion, zucchini, garlic and oregano to Dutch oven. Cook over medium-low heat 4 to 5 minutes or until onion is tender, stirring occasionally. Add vegetable mixture and remaining ingredients to slow cooker; mix well. Cover; cook on LOW 8 to 10 hours. Serve over noodles.

Favorite recipe from ***Marti Munns, Redwood City, CA***

Dad's Dill Beef Roast

Makes 6 to 8 servings

1 beef chuck roast (3 to 4 pounds)
1 large jar whole dill pickles, undrained

Place beef in slow cooker. Pour pickles with juice over top. Cover; cook on LOW 8 to 10 hours. Shred beef with two forks before serving.

Edward says: Pile this beef onto a toasted roll or bun, and you'll have an out-of-this world sandwich! Or, for an easy dinner variation, serve it with mashed potatoes.

Favorite recipe from ***Edward Felauer, Hortonville, WI***

Black-Eyed Roast

Makes 6 servings

1 beef rump roast (about 3 pounds)
1½ teaspoons garlic pepper
1 teaspoon salt
1 can (14½ ounces) black-eyed peas, drained
1 can (about 15 ounces) sliced potatoes, drained
6 cloves garlic
½ cup water
1 packet (3 ounces) gravy mix
1 tablespoon granulated beef bouillon

1. Sprinkle roast with garlic pepper and salt. Place in slow cooker. Add peas, potatoes and garlic.

2. Combine water, gravy mix and bouillon in small bowl; mix well. Pour over roast.

3. Cover; cook on LOW 8 to 10 hours.

Favorite recipe from ***Kat Minnick, Tehachapi, CA***

Beef with Mushroom and Red Wine Gravy

Makes 6 servings

1½ pounds well-trimmed beef for stew, cut into 1-inch cubes
2 medium onions, cut into ½-inch wedges
1 package (8 ounces) sliced baby button, cremini or other fresh mushrooms
1 package (1 ounce) dry beefy-onion soup mix
3 tablespoons cornstarch
⅛ teaspoon salt
⅛ teaspoon black pepper
1½ cups dry red wine

Place beef, onions and mushrooms in slow cooker. Sprinkle with soup mix, cornstarch, salt and pepper. Pour wine over all. Cover; cook on LOW 10 to 12 hours or on HIGH 5 to 6 hours.

Anne says: It's like beef bourguignon...without the fat.

Favorite recipe from ***Anne Colville Roberts, Bellville, WI***

pork suppers

Sweet 'n' Spicy Ribs

Makes 10 servings

5 cups barbecue sauce*
¾ cup brown sugar
¼ cup honey
2 tablespoons Cajun seasoning
1 tablespoon garlic powder
1 tablespoon onion powder
6 pounds pork or beef back ribs, cut into 3-rib portions

**NOTE: Barbecue sauce adds a significant flavor to this recipe. Use your favorite sauce to ensure you fully enjoy the dish.*

1. Combine barbecue sauce, brown sugar, honey, Cajun seasoning, garlic powder and onion powder in medium bowl. Remove 1 cup mixture; refrigerate and reserve for dipping sauce.

2. Place ribs in large slow cooker. Pour barbecue sauce mixture over ribs. Cover; cook on LOW 8 hours or until meat is very tender.

3. Uncover; remove ribs. Skim fat from sauce. Serve ribs with reserved dipping sauce.

Tawnie says: This dish is excellent over rice.

Favorite recipe from ***Tawnie Goodwin, Saegertown, PA***

Sweet 'n' Spicy Ribs

Pork & Tomato Ragout

Makes 6 servings

2 pounds pork for stew, cut into 1-inch pieces
¼ cup all-purpose flour
3 tablespoons oil
1¼ cups white wine
2 pounds red potatoes, cut into ½-inch pieces
1 can (14½ ounces) diced tomatoes, undrained
1 cup finely chopped onion
1 cup water
½ cup finely chopped celery
2 cloves garlic, minced
½ teaspoon black pepper
1 cinnamon stick
3 tablespoons chopped fresh parsley

1. Toss pork with flour. Heat oil in large skillet over medium-high heat. Add pork to skillet and brown on all sides. Place pork in slow cooker.

2. Add wine to skillet; bring to a boil, scraping up browned bits from bottom of skillet. Pour into slow cooker.

3. Add all remaining ingredients except parsley. Cover; cook on LOW 6 to 8 hours or until pork and potatoes are tender. Remove and discard cinnamon stick. Adjust seasonings, if desired. Sprinkle with parsley just before serving.

Pork & Tomato Ragout

Pork Tenderloin with Thyme and White Beans

Makes 10 to 12 servings

- **2 to 3 pork tenderloins (2 to 3 pounds) *or* 1 boneless pork top loin roast (3 to 4 pounds)**
- **1 head garlic, separated into cloves and peeled**
- **Salt**
- **White pepper**
- **2 cups navy beans, soaked overnight**
- **1 cup red wine**
- **¾ cup white wine**
- **¼ cup hot water**
- **2 tablespoons dried thyme leaves**
- **2 teaspoons dried oregano leaves**
- **1 teaspoon chopped garlic**
- **1 teaspoon baking soda**
- **2 yellow onions, quartered**
- **1 medium leek, cut into ⅛-inch-thick slices**
- **1 tablespoon olive oil**
- **1 tablespoon unsalted butter, melted**

1. With a paring knife, poke holes about 1 inch deep evenly around tenderloins. Push 1 peeled garlic clove into each hole. Season to taste with salt and white pepper.

2. Drain beans; place in slow cooker. Add wines, water, thyme, oregano, garlic and baking soda; mix well. Top with onions, leek and pork. Combine oil and butter in small bowl; pour over pork.

3. Cover; cook on LOW 6 to 8 hours or until beans are tender and internal temperature of pork reaches 165°F when tested with meat thermometer inserted into thickest part of tenderloin.

Favorite recipe from ***Amparo Orban, Fairfield, CT***

Lemon Pork Chops

Makes 4 servings

1 tablespoon vegetable oil
4 boneless pork chops
3 cans (8 ounces each) tomato sauce
1 large onion, quartered and sliced (optional)
1 large green bell pepper, cut into strips
1 tablespoon lemon-pepper seasoning
1 tablespoon Worcestershire sauce
1 large lemon, quartered

1. Heat oil in large skillet over medium-low heat. Brown pork chops on both sides. Drain excess fat. Place pork in slow cooker.

2. Combine tomato sauce, onion, if desired, bell pepper, lemon-pepper seasoning and Worcestershire sauce in slow cooker. Squeeze juice from lemon quarters over mixture; drop squeezed peels into slow cooker. Cover; cook on LOW 6 to 8 hours or until pork is tender.

Ginger says: Serve with rolls, green beans and mashed potatoes. Use the spiced-up tomato sauce for gravy on the potatoes. (If you like, add an extra can of tomato sauce to the slow cooker for even more gravy.) This makes an excellent meal!

Favorite recipe from ***Ginger Williams, Lauderdale, MS***

Hearty White Beans and Ham

Makes 10 servings

1 package (16 ounces) dried navy beans or mixed dried beans
Water
1 meaty ham bone
1 can (14½ ounces) tomatoes with green chilies, undrained
1 medium potato, diced
1 rib celery, diced
½ small onion, diced
½ (1-ounce) package dry onion soup mix
1 tablespoon Worcestershire sauce
1 teaspoon salt
½ teaspoon black pepper

1. Sort, rinse and drain beans. Place in Dutch oven; cover with water. Bring to a boil; reduce heat and simmer 1 hour. Drain water; return beans to Dutch oven. Add ham bone and enough water to cover generously. Cook 1 to 2 hours over low heat. Remove ham bone; pull meat from bone.

2. Transfer beans, liquid, ham bone and meat to slow cooker. Add remaining ingredients; mix well. Cover; cook on LOW 6 to 8 hours or until beans are tender. Remove and discard ham bone.

Kathy says: Taste at some point during cooking for spices; if ham is very salty, no more salt may be needed.

Favorite recipe from ***Kathy Baldwin, Pulaski, TN***

Bar Lazy D Barbecued Pork and Beans

Makes 8 servings

- **2 pounds pork for stew, cut into 1-inch cubes**
- **½ cup chopped onion**
- **1 bottle (12 to 16 ounces) barbecue sauce, divided**
- **2 cans (16 ounces each) baked beans, drained**
- **1 can (14½ ounces) chopped tomatoes, undrained**
- **½ cup packed brown sugar**
- **¼ teaspoon chili powder**
- **¼ teaspoon cayenne pepper**

1. Combine pork, onion and 1 cup barbecue sauce in slow cooker. Cover; cook on HIGH 4 to 5 hours or on LOW 6 to 8 hours or until pork is tender.

2. Add remaining barbecue sauce, baked beans, tomatoes, brown sugar and chili powder; mix well. Cover; cook on HIGH 30 minutes or until mixture is warmed through.

Favorite recipe from ***Lynnette Davids, Wichita Falls, TX***

Two White Meats Together (Marinated Pork and Chicken)

Makes 12 servings

- **6 pounds boneless chicken pieces**
- **2 pounds lean boneless pork, cubed**
- **6 cups beef broth**
- **2 cups sherry or apple juice**
- **6 Roma tomatoes, chopped**
- **4 cloves garlic, crushed**
- **2 teaspoons salt**
- **1 teaspoon dried rosemary leaves**
- **1 teaspoon black pepper**

1. Place chicken and pork in large bowl. To make marinade, combine remaining ingredients in large bowl. Pour ½ of marinade mixture over chicken and pork. Cover meat; marinate in refrigerator 4 hours or overnight. Cover remaining marinade; refrigerate.

2. Drain and discard marinade from meats. Place meats in slow cooker. Add remaining fresh marinade. Cover; cook on LOW 6 to 8 hours or until meat is tender. Adjust seasonings, if desired.

Favorite recipe from ***David Zorich, Hilliard, OH***

Sweet Kraut Chops

Makes 6 to 8 servings

3 pounds bone-in pork rib chops
½ teaspoon garlic powder
½ teaspoon black pepper
1 bag (32 ounces) sauerkraut
1 cup applesauce

1. Place pork chops in slow cooker. Sprinkle with garlic powder and pepper. Pour sauerkraut and applesauce over pork.

2. Cover; cook on LOW 6 to 8 hours or until pork is tender.

Favorite recipe from ***Rhonda Peterson, Villa Park, IL***

Sauerkraut Pork Ribs

Makes 12 servings

1 tablespoon vegetable oil
3 to 4 pounds pork country-style ribs
1 large onion, thinly sliced
1 teaspoon caraway seeds
½ teaspoon garlic powder
¼ to ½ teaspoon black pepper
¾ cup water
1 jar (about 28 ounces) sauerkraut
6 medium potatoes, quartered

1. Heat oil in large skillet over medium-low heat. Brown ribs on all sides; transfer ribs to slow cooker. Drain excess fat.

2. Add onion to skillet; cook and stir until tender. Add caraway seeds, garlic powder and pepper; cook 15 minutes. Transfer onion mixture to slow cooker.

3. Add water to skillet and scrape bottom of pan. Pour pan juices into slow cooker. Partially drain sauerkraut, leaving some liquid; pour over meat in slow cooker. Top with potatoes. Cover; cook on LOW 6 to 8 hours or until potatoes are tender, stirring once during cooking.

Favorite recipe from ***Chris Brill, Shorewood, WI***

Sweet Kraut Chops

soups & stews

Beef Stew

Makes 8 servings

- **3 pounds beef for stew, cut into 1½-inch cubes**
- **5 carrots, cut into bite-size pieces**
- **5 potatoes, diced**
- **4 onions, quartered**
- **2 stalks celery, chopped**
- **1 can (about 28 ounces) diced tomatoes, undrained**
- **1½ cups water**
- **1½ tablespoons salt**
- **1½ teaspoons paprika**
- **1½ teaspoons Worcestershire sauce**
- **¾ teaspoon black pepper**
- **1 clove garlic, minced**
- **1 bay leaf**

1. Place beef, carrots, potatoes, onions, celery and tomatoes with juice in slow cooker. Blend water with spices in medium bowl. Add to slow cooker; stir to combine.

2. Cover; cook on LOW 10 to 12 hours. Stir occasionally. Remove and discard bay leaf before serving. Garnish as desired.

Favorite recipe from ***Richard White, Lewistown, PA***

Beef Stew

Cajun Chili

Makes 10 servings

1½ pounds ground beef
2 cans (15 ounces each) Cajun-style mixed vegetables, undrained
2 cans (10¾ ounces each) condensed tomato soup, undiluted
1 can (14½ ounces) diced tomatoes, undrained
3 sausages with Cheddar cheese (about 8 ounces), quartered and sliced into bite-size pieces
Shredded cheddar cheese (optional)

1. Cook and stir ground beef in medium skillet over medium-high heat until no longer pink. Drain well.

2. Place ground beef, mixed vegetables, tomato soup, tomatoes and sausages in slow cooker. Cover; cook on HIGH 2 hours.

3. Serve with shredded cheese, if desired.

Favorite recipe from ***Jillian A. Walker, Alcolu, SC***

Cajun Chili

Chicken & Barley Soup

Makes 4 servings

- **1 cup thinly sliced celery**
- **1 medium onion, coarsely chopped**
- **1 carrot, cut into thin slices**
- **½ cup uncooked medium pearled barley**
- **1 clove garlic, minced**
- **1 cut-up whole chicken (about 3 pounds)**
- **1 tablespoon olive oil**
- **2½ cups chicken broth**
- **1 can (14½ ounces) diced tomatoes, undrained**
- **¾ teaspoon salt**
- **½ teaspoon dried basil leaves**
- **¼ teaspoon black pepper**

1. Place celery, onion, carrot, barley and garlic in slow cooker.

2. Remove and discard skin from chicken pieces. Separate drumsticks from thighs. Trim back bone from breasts. Save wings for another use.

3. Heat oil in large skillet over medium-high heat; brown chicken pieces on all sides. Place chicken in slow cooker.

4. Add broth, tomatoes with juice, salt, basil and pepper to slow cooker. Cover; cook on LOW 7 to 8 hours or on HIGH 4 hours or until chicken and barley are tender.

5. Remove chicken from slow cooker. Separate chicken from bones. Discard bones. Cut chicken into bite-size pieces; stir into soup.

Favorite recipe from ***Susan Richardson, Libertyville, IL***

Bobbie's Vegetable Hamburger Soup

Makes 4 servings

- **1 teaspoon vegetable oil**
- **1 pound 95% lean ground beef**
- **2 cans (14½ ounces each) seasoned diced tomatoes, undrained**
- **1 package (16 ounces) frozen vegetable blend**
- **2 cups water**
- **1 can (10¾ ounces) condensed tomato soup, undiluted**
- **1 package (1 ounce) dry onion soup mix**
- **1 teaspoon sugar**

1. Heat oil in large skillet over medium-low heat. Add beef; cook and stir until no longer pink. Drain fat.

2. Place beef and remaining ingredients in slow cooker; stir to combine. Cover; cook on LOW 6 to 8 hours.

Jan says: Try this with ground turkey, too!

Favorite recipe from ***Jan Davis, Minneapolis, MN***

Pea-Cadilly Chili

Makes 8 servings

- **1 pound pork sausage, casings removed**
- **1 pound smoked pork sausage, cut into ¼-inch slices**
- **1 cup chopped onion**
- **1 cup chopped bell pepper**
- **½ cup brown sugar**
- **2 cans (14 ounces each) black-eyed peas, rinsed and drained**
- **1 can (14 ounces) pinto beans, rinsed and drained**
- **1 can (14 ounces) pinto beans with jalapeño peppers, undrained**
- **¼ cup Worcestershire sauce**
- **2 teaspoons dry mustard**

1. Combine sausages, onion and pepper in large skillet over medium-high heat. Cook and stir 5 minutes or until sausage is no longer pink.

2. Add sausage mixture and remaining ingredients to slow cooker; stir to combine. Cover; cook on LOW 8 hours.

Favorite recipe from ***Rosanne Massey-Chastain, Bullard, TX***

Summer Squash Stew

Makes 6 servings

4 cans (14½ ounces each) diced seasoned tomatoes
2 pounds cooked Italian turkey sausage or diced cooked chicken
5 medium yellow summer squash, thinly sliced
5 medium zucchini, thinly sliced
1 red onion, finely chopped
2 tablespoons dried Italian herb mix
1 tablespoon dried tomato, basil and garlic salt-free spice mix
4 cups (16 ounces) shredded Mexican cheese blend

1. Combine all ingredients except cheese in slow cooker. Cover; cook on LOW 3 hours.

2. Top stew with cheese and cook an additional 15 minutes or until cheese melts.

Favorite recipe from ***Kristin A. Drake, Attica, NY***

Easy Chili

Makes 4 servings

1 teaspoon vegetable oil
1 pound 95% lean ground beef
1 medium onion, chopped
2 cans (10¾ ounces each) condensed tomato soup, undiluted
1 cup water
Salt
Black pepper
Chili powder

1. Heat oil in large skillet over medium-high heat. Brown beef and onion. Drain excess fat.

2. Place meat mixture, soup, water, salt, pepper and chili powder to taste in slow cooker. Cover; cook on LOW 6 hours.

Pam says: I've left it cooking for 8 hours without a problem. Garnish with shredded cheese and serve with crackers or thick slices of Italian bread.

Favorite recipe from ***Pam Britt, Johnstown, PA***

Summer Squash Stew

Potato & Spinach Soup with Gouda

Makes 8 to 10 servings

SOUP

- **9 medium Yukon Gold potatoes, peeled and cubed (about 6 cups)**
- **2 cans (14½ ounces each) chicken broth**
- **½ cup water**
- **1 small red onion, finely diced**
- **5 ounces baby spinach leaves**
- **½ teaspoon salt**
- **¼ teaspoon ground red pepper**
- **¼ teaspoon black pepper**
- **2½ cups shredded smoked Gouda cheese, divided**
- **1 can (12 ounces) evaporated milk**

GARNISH

- **¼ cup olive oil**
- **4 cloves garlic, cut into thin slices**
- **5 to 7 sprigs parsley, finely chopped**

1. Combine potatoes, chicken broth, water, red onion, spinach, salt, red pepper and black pepper in slow cooker. Cover; cook on LOW 10 hours or until potatoes are tender.

2. Slightly mash potatoes in slow cooker; add 2 cups smoked Gouda and evaporated milk. Cover; cook on HIGH 15 to 20 minutes or until cheese is melted.

3. Heat olive oil in small saucepan over low heat until hot. Add garlic; cook and stir until golden brown. Set aside. Pour soup into bowls. Sprinkle 2 to 3 teaspoons remaining Gouda cheese into each bowl. Top with spoonful of garlic. Garnish with parsley.

Paula says: After many experiments, I made a family recipe for potato soup a little more exotic by adding the buttery, smoky flavor of Gouda cheese and a slight "kick" from cayenne pepper. This soup goes well with simple fish dinners, or you can add ham and serve it as an entire meal. If you add ham, eliminate the salt in the recipe. Enjoy!

Favorite recipe from ***Paula Murphy, Crystal Lake, IL***

Potato & Spinach Soup with Gouda

Poor Man's Stew

Makes 8 servings

- **2 cans (14½ ounces each) chopped tomatoes with Italian seasoning**
- **1 can (15 ounces) red kidney beans, drained**
- **1 can (15 ounces) black beans, drained**
- **1 can (15 ounces) chick-peas, drained**
- **1 can (14 ounces) green beans, drained**
- **1 can (11 ounces) whole kernel corn, drained**
- **½ pound cooked Polish or Italian sausage, diced**
- **1 cup hot water**
- **2 chicken bouillon cubes**
- **2 teaspoons minced garlic**
- **½ teaspoon garlic salt**
- **½ teaspoon dried basil leaves**
- **½ teaspoon black pepper**

Place all ingredients in slow cooker. Cover; cook on HIGH 3 hours.

Tyla says: Serve this stew over pasta and top with grated Parmesan cheese.

Favorite recipe from ***Tyla Morris, Lighthouse Point, FL***

Chili with Turkey & Beans

Makes 4 servings

2 cans (14½ ounces each) whole peeled tomatoes, drained
2 cans (15 ounces each) red kidney beans, rinsed and drained
1 pound cooked ground turkey
1 can (15 ounces) black beans, rinsed and drained
1 can (12 ounces) tomato sauce
1 cup finely chopped onion
1 cup finely chopped celery
1 cup finely chopped carrot
½ cup Amaretto liqueur (optional)
3 tablespoons chili powder
4 teaspoons cumin
1 tablespoon Worcestershire sauce
2 teaspoons ground red pepper
1 teaspoon salt

Combine all ingredients in slow cooker. Cover; cook on HIGH 7 hours.

Adrian says: For a thicker sauce, leave the cover off your cooker for the last hour. Serve with shredded cheese or cornbread, or by itself!

Favorite recipe from ***Adrian Lewis, Woodbury, CT***

Beef Fajita Soup

Makes 8 servings

- 1 pound beef for stew
- 1 can (15 ounces) pinto beans, rinsed and drained
- 1 can (15 ounces) black beans, rinsed and drained
- 1 can (14½ ounces) diced tomatoes with roasted garlic, undrained
- 1 can (14½ ounces) beef broth
- 1 small green bell pepper, thinly sliced
- 1 small red bell pepper, thinly sliced
- 1 small onion, thinly sliced
- 1½ cups water
- 2 teaspoons ground cumin
- 1 teaspoon seasoned salt
- 1 teaspoon black pepper
- Toppings: sour cream, shredded Monterey Jack or Cheddar cheese, chopped olives

1. Combine all ingredients except toppings in slow cooker.

2. Cover; cook on LOW 8 hours or until beef is tender. Serve with suggested toppings.

Candace says: This soup is excellent served with a crusty loaf of brown bread.

Favorite recipe from ***Candace Morse, Midwest City, OK***

Beef Fajita Soup

Chili

Makes 6 servings

3 pounds ground beef
2 cans (14½ ounces each) diced tomatoes, undrained
2 cans (14½ ounces each) chili beans, undrained
2 cups sliced onions
1 can (12 ounces) corn, drained
1 cup chopped green bell pepper
1 can (15 ounces) tomato sauce
3 tablespoons chili powder
1 teaspoon garlic powder
½ teaspoon cumin
½ teaspoon dried oregano leaves

1. Cook and stir beef in large skillet over medium-high heat until no longer pink. Drain fat. Transfer beef to slow cooker.

2. Add remaining ingredients to slow cooker; stir to combine. Cover; cook on LOW 4 hours.

Favorite recipe from ***Sue Lineberry, Concord, NC***

Chili

Quickie Vegetable-Beef Soup

Makes 10 servings

1 tablespoon vegetable oil
1 to 2 pounds beef for stew
3 cans (15 ounces each) mixed vegetables
2 cans (10¾ ounces each) condensed golden mushroom soup, undiluted
1 can (14½ ounces) stewed tomatoes
1 beef bouillon cube
1 tablespoon Worcestershire sauce
1 medium onion, chopped
Salt
Black pepper
1 bay leaf

1. Heat oil in large skillet over medium-low heat; brown beef on all sides. Drain fat. Transfer beef to slow cooker.

2. Add remaining ingredients to slow cooker; mix thoroughly. Cover; cook on LOW 6 to 8 hours. Removed and discard bay leaf.

Favorite recipe from ***Susan Christensen, Lakewood, CO***

Curried Beef Stew

Makes 3 servings

1 pound beef for stew
3 medium white potatoes, peeled and cut into bite-size pieces
1 can (12 ounces) tomato paste
½ onion, diced
½ yellow bell pepper, chopped
½ red bell pepper, chopped
½ green bell pepper, chopped
1 tablespoon curry powder
½ teaspoon black pepper

Place all ingredients in slow cooker. Cover; cook on HIGH 4 to 6 hours.

Favorite recipe from ***Velda Arthur, Winston-Salem, NC***

Slow Cooker Green Chili Stew

Makes 8 to 10 servings

1 pork roast (about 4 pounds)
1 potato, peeled and diced
Garlic salt
1 can (28 ounces) stewed tomatoes
1 cup chopped onion
1 cup chopped celery
1 cup chopped green bell pepper
2 cans (4 ounces each) diced mild green chilies, drained
1 can (4 ounces) diced hot green chilies, drained

1. Place pork and potato in slow cooker. Season with garlic salt. Add water to cover. Cover; cook on LOW 8 to 10 hours.

2. Shred pork. Add tomatoes, onion, celery, bell pepper and chilies to slow cooker. Cover; cook on LOW 6 hours.

Favorite recipe from ***Judy McDonald, Mt. Tabor, NJ***

dips & sauces

Slow Cooker Cheese Dip

Makes 16 to 18 servings

1 pound ground beef
1 pound Italian sausage
1 package (1 pound) processed cheese, cubed
1 can (11 ounces) sliced jalapeño peppers, drained
1 medium onion, diced
½ pound Cheddar cheese, cubed
1 package (8 ounces) cream cheese, cubed
1 container (8 ounces) cottage cheese
1 container (8 ounces) sour cream
1 can (8 ounces) diced tomatoes, drained
3 cloves garlic, minced
Salt
Black pepper

1. Cook and stir ground beef and sausage in medium skillet over medium-high heat until no longer pink. Drain fat. Transfer beef and sausage mixture to slow cooker.

2. Add processed cheese, jalapeño peppers, onion, Cheddar cheese, cream cheese, cottage cheese, sour cream, tomatoes and garlic to slow cooker. Season to taste with salt and pepper. Cover; cook on HIGH 1½ to 2 hours or until cheeses are melted. Serve with crackers or tortilla chips.

Favorite recipe from ***Judy McDonald, Mt. Tabor, NJ***

Slow Cooker Cheese Dip

Chunky Pinto Bean Dip

Makes about 5 cups dip

2 cans (15 ounces each) pinto beans, rinsed and drained
1 can (14½ ounces) Mexican-style diced tomatoes, drained
1 cup chopped onion
⅔ cup chunky salsa
1 tablespoon vegetable oil
1½ teaspoons minced garlic
1 teaspoon ground coriander
1 teaspoon ground cumin
1½ cups (6 ounces) shredded Mexican cheese blend or shredded Cheddar cheese
¼ cup chopped cilantro
Blue corn or other tortilla chips
Assorted raw vegetables

1. Combine beans, tomatoes, onion, salsa, oil, garlic, coriander and cumin in slow cooker. Cover; cook on LOW 5 to 6 hours or until onion is tender.

2. Partially mash bean mixture with potato masher. Stir in cheese and cilantro. Serve at room temperature with chips and vegetables. Top with sour cream and garnish, if desired.

Chunky Pinto Bean Dip

Spaghetti Sauce

Makes 6 servings

1 tablespoon olive oil
1½ pounds ground beef
1 medium onion, chopped
1 medium green bell pepper, diced
2 cans (28 ounces each) crushed tomatoes, undrained
1 can (15 ounces) beef broth
1 can (8 ounces) tomato sauce
1 can (6 ounces) tomato paste (or more to taste)
½ cup grated Parmesan cheese
1 tablespoon brown sugar
2 teaspoons garlic powder
1 teaspoon dried oregano leaves
1 teaspoon dried basil leaves

1. Heat oil in large skillet over medium-low heat. Add ground beef, onion and bell pepper. Cook, stirring frequently, until meat is no longer pink and onion is tender. Drain fat.

2. Place meat mixture in slow cooker. Add remaining ingredients; stir thoroughly. Cover; cook on LOW 6 to 8 hours.

Favorite recipe from ***Sandra Innis, Peabody, MA***

Chicken & Shrimp Sauce

Makes 6 servings

- **1 jar (28 ounces) spaghetti sauce**
- **1 pound boneless skinless chicken breasts, cut into small pieces**
- **6 cooked medium shrimp**
- **1 cup sliced mushrooms**
- **1 medium green bell pepper, chopped**
- **1 medium red bell pepper, chopped**
- **1 onion, chopped**
- **2 cloves garlic, minced**
- **1 tablespoon olive oil**
- **½ teaspoon dried oregano leaves**

Combine all ingredients in slow cooker. Cover; cook on LOW 8 hours.

Rose says: Serve this sauce over white rice.

Favorite recipe from ***Rose Anderson-Wise, Catonsville, MD***

Sausage Dip

Makes 20 servings

1 pound bulk sausage, cooked
1 pound processed American cheese
1 pound Mexican-flavored processed cheese
1 can (16 ounces) refried beans
1 can (10¾ ounces) condensed cream of mushroom soup, undiluted
1 small onion, chopped
Tortilla chips

Place all ingredients except tortilla chips in slow cooker. Cover; cook on LOW about 2 hours or until heated through.

Elissa says: Serve with tortilla chips!

Favorite recipe from ***Elissa Stodolak, Grove City, PA***

Creamy Cheesy Spinach Dip

Makes about 4 cups dip

2 packages (10 ounces each) frozen chopped spinach, thawed
2 cups chopped onions
1 teaspoon salt
½ teaspoon garlic powder
¼ teaspoon black pepper
12 ounces processed cheese with jalapeño peppers, cubed
Assorted crackers (optional)
Cherry tomatoes with pulp removed (optional)

1. Drain spinach and squeeze dry, reserving ¾ cup liquid. Place spinach, reserved liquid, onions, salt, garlic powder and pepper in slow cooker; stir to blend. Cover; cook on HIGH 1½ hours.

2. Stir in cheese and cook 30 minutes longer or until melted. Serve with crackers or fill cherry tomato shells, if desired.

Reuben Dip

Makes 12 servings

- 1 jar or bag (about 32 ounces) sauerkraut, drained
- 2 cups shredded Swiss cheese
- 3 packages (2½ ounces each) corned beef, shredded
- ½ cup (1 stick) margarine, melted
- 1 egg, beaten
- Rye cocktail bread or crackers

1. Combine all ingredients except rye bread in slow cooker. Cover; cook on HIGH 2 hours.

2. Serve with rye cocktail bread.

Favorite recipe from ***Dot Lindsey, Harrison, OH***

Sauce for Cabbage Rolls

Makes 16 servings

- 3 cans (10¾ ounces each) condensed cheese soup, undiluted
- 1 can (10¾ ounces) condensed tomato soup, undiluted
- 2½ cups reserved cabbage water (page 92)

Combine all ingredients in medium saucepan. Cook, stirring occasionally, over medium heat until warm.

Favorite recipe from ***Shirley McLear, Manistique, MI***

Mom's Spaghetti Sauce

Makes 10 to 12 servings

7½ cups water
3 cans (15 ounces each) tomato purée
3 cans (6 ounces each) tomato paste*
1 can (14½ ounces) tomatoes, undrained
2 large onions, chopped
3 tablespoons sugar
2 tablespoons salt
1½ tablespoons Italian seasoning
1½ tablespoons dried oregano leaves
6 large cloves garlic, minced
1 tablespoon black pepper
3 bay leaves
2 to 2½ pounds Italian hot or sweet sausage (optional)
3 pounds ground beef, shaped into about 35 meatballs and browned (optional)

**Note: You may want to add more tomato paste if sauce is not thick enough for your taste.*

1. Add all ingredients except sausage and meatballs to slow cooker; mix well. If using sausage and meatballs, prepare sauce in two slow cookers.

2. Cover; cook on HIGH 1 hour. Add meatballs and sausages to slow cookers, if desired. Cover; cook on LOW 6 to 8 hours.

Lynda says: Serve over hot spaghetti or your favorite pasta. Any leftover meatless sauce can be served over cooked boneless, skinless chicken breasts or used to make a flavorful base for a pot of vegetable soup.

Favorite recipe from ***Lynda McCormick, Burkburnett, TX***

Mom's Spaghetti Sauce

Pizza Fondue

Makes 20 to 25 appetizer servings

- **½ pound bulk Italian sausage**
- **1 cup chopped onion**
- **2 jars (26 ounces each) meatless spaghetti sauce**
- **4 ounces thinly sliced ham, finely chopped**
- **1 package (3 ounces) sliced pepperoni, finely chopped**
- **¼ teaspoon red pepper flakes**
- **1 pound mozzarella cheese, cut into ¾-inch cubes**
- **1 loaf Italian or French bread, cut into 1-inch cubes**

1. Cook sausage and onion in large skillet until sausage is browned. Drain off fat.

2. Transfer sausage mixture to slow cooker. Stir in spaghetti sauce, ham, pepperoni and red pepper flakes. Cover; cook on LOW 3 to 4 hours.

3. Serve sauce with cheese cubes and bread cubes.

Pizza Fondue

Bacon & Cheese Dip

Makes 16 servings (about 4 cups)

2 packages (8 ounces each) reduced-fat cream cheese, softened and cut into cubes
4 cups (16 ounces) shredded reduced-fat sharp Cheddar cheese
1 cup evaporated skimmed milk
2 tablespoons prepared yellow mustard
1 tablespoon chopped onion
2 teaspoons Worcestershire sauce
½ teaspoon salt
¼ teaspoon hot pepper sauce
1 pound turkey bacon, crisp-cooked and crumbled

1. Place cream cheese, Cheddar cheese, evaporated milk, mustard, onion, Worcestershire sauce, salt and pepper sauce in slow cooker. Cover; cook, stirring occasionally, on LOW 1 hour or until cheese melts.

2. Stir in bacon; adjust seasonings as desired. Serve with crusty bread or fruit and vegetable dippers.

Hot Dog Sauce

Makes 12 servings

2 pounds ground beef
2 cups chopped onion
3 tablespoons chili powder
2 cups ketchup
1 can (15 ounces) tomato sauce
1 can (12 ounces) beer
¼ cup prepared mustard

1. Cook and stir ground beef and onion in medium skillet over medium-high heat until meat is browned and onion is tender. Drain fat. Stir in chili powder. Transfer mixuture to slow cooker.

2. Add ketchup, tomato sauce, beer and mustard to slow cooker; mix well. Cover; cook on LOW 3 hours.

Linda says: Serve over hot dogs and top with shredded Cheddar cheese, relish and mustard. Enjoy!

Favorite recipe from ***Linda Tate, Lexington, KY***

Easy Taco Dip

Makes about 3 cups dip

½ pound ground chuck
1 cup frozen corn
½ cup chopped onion
½ cup salsa
½ cup mild taco sauce
1 can (4 ounces) diced mild green chilies, drained
1 can (4 ounces) sliced ripe olives, drained
1 cup (4 ounces) shredded Mexican cheese blend
Tortilla chips
Sour cream

1. Cook meat in large nonstick skillet over medium-high heat until no longer pink, stirring to separate; drain. Spoon into slow cooker.

2. Add corn, onion, salsa, taco sauce, chilies and olives to slow cooker; stir to combine. Cover; cook on LOW 2 to 4 hours.

3. Just before serving, stir in cheese. Serve with tortilla chips and sour cream.

Note: To keep this dip hot throughout your entire party, simply leave it in the slow cooker on LOW.

Easy Taco Dip

rice & noodles

Chicken Pilaf

Makes 10 servings

2 pounds chopped cooked chicken
2 cans (8 ounces each) tomato sauce
2½ cups water
1⅓ cups uncooked rice
1 cup chopped onion
1 cup chopped celery
1 cup chopped green bell pepper
⅔ cup sliced black olives
¼ cup sliced almonds
¼ cup (½ stick) margarine or butter
2 cloves garlic, minced
2½ teaspoons salt
½ teaspoon ground allspice
½ teaspoon ground turmeric
¼ teaspoon curry powder
¼ teaspoon black pepper

Combine all ingredients in slow cooker; stir well. Cover; cook on LOW 6 to 9 hours or on HIGH 3 hours.

Favorite recipe from ***Sandra Marie Swift, Pensacola, FL***

Chicken Pilaf

Peppered Beef Tips

Makes 2 to 3 servings

1 pound beef round tip or round steaks
2 cloves garlic, minced
Black pepper
1 can (10¾ ounces) condensed French onion soup, undiluted
1 can (10¾ ounces) condensed cream of mushroom soup, undiluted
Hot cooked noodles or rice

Place steaks in slow cooker. Sprinkle with garlic and pepper. Pour soups over beef. Cover; cook on LOW 8 to 10 hours.

Barbara says: Serve these beef tips over cooked noodles or rice.

Favorite recipe from ***Barbara Messman, Birmingham, AL***

Peppered Beef Tips

Catch-all-tori

Makes 8 to 10 servings

2 cups uncooked pasta
2 tablespoons olive oil
2 medium onions, chopped
1½ cups sour cream
1½ cups shredded mozzarella cheese, divided
½ cup grated Parmesan cheese
Salt
Black pepper
3 to 4 cups cooked chicken or turkey, cut into bite-size pieces
3 cups spaghetti sauce
½ cup dry bread crumbs

1. Cook pasta according to package directions. Add olive oil and onions during last five minutes of cooking. Drain; cover to keep warm.

2. Combine sour cream, 1 cup mozzarella and Parmesan in medium saucepan; cook over medium heat until evenly melted, stirring occasionally.

3. Place ½ of pasta mixture in slow cooker. Top with ½ of cheese sauce. Sprinkle with salt and pepper to taste. Add ½ of chicken pieces and ½ of spaghetti sauce. Repeat all layers, ending with spaghetti sauce. Sprinkle bread crumbs and remaining ½ cup mozzarella cheese over top. Cover; cook on LOW 4 to 6 hours.

Favorite recipe from ***Sally Kennelly, Carnation, WA***

Slow Cooker Macaroni and Cheese

Makes 6 servings

1 package (16 ounces) elbow macaroni, uncooked
2 eggs
¾ cup milk
4 cups (16 ounces) grated Cheddar cheese
1 can (12 ounces) evaporated milk
1 can (10¾ ounces) condensed Cheddar cheese soup, undiluted
½ cup (1 stick) margarine or butter, melted

1. Cook macaroni according to package directions; drain. Transfer macaroni to slow cooker.

2. Combine eggs and milk in small bowl; whisk well.

3. Add egg mixture and all remaining ingredients to slow cooker with macaroni; mix well. Cover; cook on LOW 3 hours.

Favorite recipe from ***Claudia Goff, Clinton Township, MI***

Shrimp Jambalaya

Makes 6 servings

1 can (28 ounces) diced tomatoes, undrained
1 medium onion, chopped
1 medium red bell pepper, chopped
1 rib celery, chopped (about ½ cup)
2 tablespoons minced garlic
2 teaspoons dried parsley flakes
2 teaspoons dried oregano leaves
1 teaspoon hot pepper sauce
½ teaspoon dried thyme leaves
2 pounds raw large shrimp, peeled, deveined and cooked
2 cups uncooked instant rice
2 cups fat-free reduced-sodium chicken broth

1. Combine tomatoes with juice, onion, bell pepper, celery, garlic, parsley, oregano, hot pepper sauce and thyme in slow cooker. Cover; cook on LOW 8 hours or on HIGH 4 hours.

2. Stir in shrimp. Cover; cook on LOW 20 minutes.

3. Meanwhile, prepare rice according to package directions, substituting broth for water. Serve jambalaya over hot cooked rice.

Favorite recipe from ***Lucy Cannek, Elmhurst, IL***

Slow Cooker Beef & Noodles

Makes 4 to 6 servings

1 bag (12 ounces) extra-wide egg noodles, uncooked
1 can (10¾ ounces) condensed French onion soup, undiluted
1 can (10¾ ounces) condensed cream of mushroom soup, undiluted
1 to 1½ pounds beef for stew

1. Cook noodles according to package directions; drain.

2. Meanwhile, add soups and beef to slow cooker; stir well. Cover; cook on LOW 8 to 10 hours. Serve beef mixture over hot cooked noodles.

Favorite recipe from ***Laurel Adams, Butler, KY***

Fiesta Rice and Sausage

Makes 10 to 12 servings

1 teaspoon vegetable oil
2 pounds spicy Italian sausage, casings removed
2 cloves garlic, minced
2 teaspoons ground cumin
4 onions, chopped
4 green bell peppers, chopped
3 jalapeño peppers,* seeded and minced
4 cups beef broth
2 packages (6¼ ounces each) uncooked long-grain and wild rice mix

**Jalapeño peppers can sting and irritate the skin; wear rubber gloves when handling peppers and do not touch eyes. Wash hands after handling.*

1. Heat oil in large skillet over medium-high heat; cook and stir sausage about 5 minutes or until browned.

2. Add garlic and cumin to skillet with sausage; cook 30 seconds. Add onions, bell peppers and jalapeño peppers. Cook and stir until onions are tender, about 10 minutes.

3. Transfer mixture to slow cooker. Add beef broth and rice; stir well. Cover; cook on HIGH 1 to 2 hours or on LOW 4 to 6 hours.

Fiesta Rice and Sausage

Zesty Chicken & Rice Supper

Makes 3 to 4 servings

2 boneless skinless chicken breasts, cut into 1-inch pieces
2 large bell peppers, coarsely chopped
1 small onion, chopped
1 can (28 ounces) diced tomatoes, undrained
1 package (about 1 ounce) taco seasoning
1 cup uncooked white rice
1 cup water
1 teaspoon salt
1 teaspoon black pepper
1 teaspoon ground red pepper
Shredded Cheddar cheese (optional)

Combine all ingredients in slow cooker; mix well. Cover; cook on LOW 6 to 8 hours or on HIGH 3 to 4 hours.

Cortney says: Serve in chili crocks. Garnish with shredded Cheddar cheese.

Favorite recipe from ***Cortney Morford, Tuckahoe, NJ***

Goulash

Makes 8 servings

- **1 pound ground beef**
- **5 cans (8 ounces each) tomato sauce**
- **2 cans (14½ ounces each) cut green beans, liquid drained and reserved**
- **2 cans (14½ ounces each) stewed tomatoes with Italian seasonings**
- **1 package (16 ounces) frozen corn**
- **2 cans (4 ounces each) sliced mushrooms, drained**
- **1 large white onion, chopped**
- **1 teaspoon garlic powder**
- **1 teaspoon black pepper**
- **2 bay leaves**
- **1½ cups cooked rice**

1. Cook and stir ground beef in medium skillet over medium heat until browned. Drain fat.

2. Place beef and remaining ingredients except rice in slow cooker. Add reserved liquid from green beans if goulash seems too thick. Cover; cook on HIGH 45 minutes.

3. Add rice to goulash to bring it to desired consistency. Cover; cook on LOW 1 hour. Remove and discard bay leaves before serving.

Serena says: Serve with corn bread.

Favorite recipe from ***Serena Melton, Hockley, TX***

Vegetarian Lasagna

Makes 4 servings

- **1 small eggplant, sliced into ½-inch-thick rounds**
- **½ teaspoon salt**
- **2 tablespoons olive oil, divided**
- **1 tablespoon butter**
- **½ pound mushrooms, sliced**
- **1 small onion, diced**
- **1 can (26 ounces) spaghetti sauce**
- **1 teaspoon dried basil leaves**
- **1 teaspoon dried oregano leaves**
- **2 cups part-skim ricotta cheese**
- **1½ cups (6 ounces) shredded Monterey Jack cheese**
- **1 cup grated Parmesan cheese, divided**
- **1 package (8 ounces) whole wheat lasagna, cooked and drained**
- **1 medium zucchini, thinly sliced**

1. Sprinkle eggplant with salt; let rest 10 to 15 minutes. Rinse; pat dry. Brush with 1 tablespoon olive oil. Brown on both sides in medium skillet over medium heat. Set aside.

2. Heat remaining 1 tablespoon olive oil and butter in same skillet over medium heat; cook and stir mushrooms and onion until softened. Stir in spaghetti sauce, basil and oregano. Set aside.

3. Combine ricotta cheese, Monterey Jack cheese and ½ cup Parmesan cheese in medium bowl; set aside.

4. Spread ⅓ of sauce mixture onto bottom of slow cooker. Layer with ⅓ of lasagna noodles, ½ of eggplant and ½ of cheese mixture. Repeat layers once. For final layer, use remaining ⅓ of lasagna noodles, zucchini and remaining ⅓ of sauce mixture. Top with remaining ½ cup Parmesan.

5. Cover; cook on LOW 6 hours. Let sit 15 to 20 minutes before serving.

Favorite recipe from ***Cindy Van Meter, Livingston, TX***

Vegetarian Lasagna

Chicken & Rice Dish

Makes 4 servings

- **1 jar (2½ ounces) sliced dried beef**
- **4 boneless skinless chicken breasts**
- **Garlic powder**
- **½ pound bacon**
- **2 cans (10¾ ounces each) condensed cream of mushroom soup, undiluted**
- **½ cup white wine**
- **4 cups hot cooked white rice**

1. Rinse dried beef with warm water. Place beef in bottom of slow cooker.

2. Sprinkle chicken breasts with garlic powder. Wrap each chicken breast with 1 to 2 slices bacon. Place chicken in slow cooker.

3. Stir together soup and wine; pour over chicken. Cover; cook on LOW 8 hours.

4. To serve, place 1 cup rice on each plate; top with chicken breast and gravy.

Favorite recipe from ***Carol Robbins, Jacksonville, FL***

Slow-Cooked Smothered Steak

Makes 6 servings

- **⅓ cup all-purpose flour**
- **1 teaspoon garlic salt**
- **½ teaspoon black pepper**
- **1 beef chuck shoulder or top round steak (about 2 pounds), cut into strips**
- **1 large onion, sliced**
- **1 to 2 medium green bell peppers, cut into strips**
- **1 can (4 ounces) sliced mushrooms, drained**
- **¼ cup teriyaki sauce**
- **1 package (10 ounces) frozen French-style green beans**
- **Hot cooked white rice**

1. Combine flour, garlic salt and black pepper in medium bowl. Add steak strips, tossing to coat with flour mixture. Place steak in slow cooker.

2. Layer remaining ingredients except rice in slow cooker. Cover; cook on HIGH 1 hour. Reduce heat to LOW; cook 8 hours (or leave on HIGH 5 hours). Serve over rice.

Lynda says: This is a great recipe to double (use a 12-ounce can of mushrooms when doing so). It will fill a 6-quart slow cooker if doubling or a 3½-quart model if making a single recipe. The lid may touch the green beans. Don't worry about it overflowing, because the contents will settle.

Favorite recipe from ***Lynda McCormick, Burkburnett, TX***

Fusilli Pizzaiola with Turkey Meatballs

Makes 4 servings

2 cans (14½ ounces each) no-salt-added tomatoes, undrained
1 can (8 ounces) no-salt-added tomato sauce
¼ cup chopped onion
¼ cup grated carrot
2 tablespoons no-salt-added tomato paste
2 tablespoons chopped fresh basil
1 clove garlic, minced
½ teaspoon dried thyme leaves
¼ teaspoon sugar
¼ teaspoon black pepper, divided
1 bay leaf
1 pound ground turkey breast
1 egg, lightly beaten
1 tablespoon fat-free (skim) milk
¼ cup Italian-seasoned dry bread crumbs
2 tablespoons chopped fresh parsley
8 ounces uncooked fusilli or other spiral-shaped pasta

1. Combine tomatoes, tomato sauce, onion, carrot, tomato paste, basil, garlic, thyme, sugar, ⅛ teaspoon black pepper and bay leaf in slow cooker. Break up tomatoes gently with wooden spoon. Cover; cook on LOW 4½ to 5 hours.

2. About 45 minutes before end of cooking, prepare meatballs. Preheat oven to 350°F. Combine turkey, egg and milk in large bowl. Blend in bread crumbs, parsley and remaining ⅛ teaspoon black pepper. With wet hands, shape mixture into small balls. Spray baking sheet with nonstick cooking spray. Arrange meatballs on baking sheet. Bake 25 minutes or until no longer pink in centers.

3. Add meatballs to slow cooker. Cover; cook 45 minutes to 1 hour or until meatballs are heated through. Discard bay leaf.

4. Prepare pasta according to package directions. Drain. Place in serving bowl; top with meatballs and sauce.

Favorite Brand Name™

THE BEST SLOW COOKER RECIPES

Contents

beef medley

Best Beef Brisket Ever

Makes 12 servings

1 to 2 beef briskets (about 5 pounds total)
2 cups apple cider, divided
1 head garlic, cloves separated, peeled and crushed
2 tablespoons whole peppercorns
2 tablespoons dried thyme leaves *or* ¼ cup plus 2 tablespoons fresh thyme
1 tablespoon mustard seed
1 tablespoon Cajun seasoning
1 teaspoon ground allspice
1 teaspoon ground cumin
1 teaspoon celery seed
2 to 4 whole cloves
1 bottle (12 ounces) dark beer
Sandwich rolls

1. Place brisket, ⅓ cup cider, garlic, peppercorns, thyme, mustard seed, Cajun seasoning, allspice, cumin, celery seed and cloves in large resealable plastic food storage bag. Seal bag. Turn to coat beef. Refrigerate overnight.

2. Transfer brisket and marinade to slow cooker. Add remaining 1⅔ cups apple cider and beer. Cover; cook on LOW 10 hours. Serve juices over meat on sandwich rolls. Top meat with cheese, if desired.

Suzy says: Just in time for St. Patrick's Day—or any time you crave a moist and tender corned beef sandwich—this one's an all-time favorite around my house!

Favorite recipe from ***Suzy Weaver, Costa Mesa, CA***

Best Beef Brisket Ever

Slow Cooker Pizza Casserole

Makes 6 servings

1 pound corkscrew pasta, uncooked
1½ pounds ground beef
1 pound pork sausage
4 jars (14 ounces each) prepared pizza sauce
2 cups (8 ounces) shredded mozzarella cheese
2 cups freshly grated Parmesan cheese
2 cans (4 ounces each) mushroom stems and pieces, drained
2 packages (3 ounces each) sliced pepperoni
½ cup finely chopped onion
½ cup finely chopped green bell pepper
1 clove garlic, minced

1. Prepare pasta according to package directions; drain. Set aside.

2. Meanwhile, heat large nonstick skillet over medium-high heat. Add beef and sausage. Cook and stir 7 to 8 minutes or until browned. Drain fat. Transfer meat mixture to slow cooker.

3. Add pasta and all remaining ingredients to slow cooker. Cover; cook on HIGH 2 hours or on LOW 4 hours.

Julie says: This is a great dish for potlucks and large gatherings.

*Favorite recipe from **Julie Veith, Wichita, KS***

Slow Cooker Pizza Casserole

Sloppy Slow Cooker Meat Loaf

Makes 6 servings

½ cup ketchup, divided
2 pounds ground beef
1 can (10¾ ounces) condensed cream of onion soup, undiluted
½ cup uncooked stuffing mix
⅓ cup chopped onion
2 eggs, beaten
1 teaspoon minced jalapeño pepper*
1 clove garlic, minced
½ teaspoon salt
½ teaspoon dry mustard
½ teaspoon black pepper

**Jalapeño peppers can sting and irritate the skin. Wear gloves when handling peppers and do not touch eyes. Wash hands after handling.*

Reserve 2 tablespoons ketchup. Combine all remaining ingredients, including remaining 6 tablespoons ketchup, in slow cooker; mix well. Top with reserved 2 tablespoons ketchup. Cover; cook on LOW 8 to 10 hours.

Favorite recipe from ***Daniel D. Ryan, Indianapolis, IN***

Steak and Gravy

Makes 6 to 8 servings

3 pounds beef round steak, cut into bite-size pieces
1 can (10¾ ounces) condensed cream of mushroom soup, undiluted
1¼ cups water
1 package (1 ounce) dry onion soup mix
Hot cooked egg noodles (optional)

Combine all ingredients in slow cooker. Cover; cook on LOW 8 to 10 hours. Stir before serving. Serve over egg noodles, if desired.

Favorite recipe from ***Sharon Sessa, Gulf Breeze, FL***

Country-Style Steak

Makes 4 to 6 servings

4 to 6 beef cubed steaks (about 1 to 1½ pounds)
All-purpose flour
1 tablespoon vegetable oil
1 package (1 ounce) dry onion soup mix
1 package (1 ounce) brown gravy mix
Water

1. Dust steaks with flour. Heat oil in large skillet over medium-low heat until hot. Brown steaks on both sides. Drain fat. Transfer steaks to slow cooker.

2. Add soup and gravy mixes and enough water to cover meat. Cover; cook on LOW 6 to 8 hours.

Margie says: This steak is very tender and good. Serve it with mashed potatoes.

Favorite recipe from ***Margie Kirkman, High Point, NC***

Italian Pot Roast

Makes 6 to 8 servings

1 boneless beef chuck shoulder roast (2 to 3 pounds)
1 can (28 ounces) crushed tomatoes *or* 6 to 8 fresh plum tomatoes, chopped
1 package (1 ounce) dry spaghetti sauce seasoning mix
1 teaspoon minced garlic *or* ½ teaspoon garlic powder
1 teaspoon Italian seasoning
1 package (16 ounces) spaghetti or other pasta, cooked according to package directions
Grated Parmesan cheese

1. Place all ingredients except spaghetti and cheese in slow cooker. Cover; cook on HIGH 5 to 6 hours.

2. Serve sliced roast over hot cooked spaghetti. Sprinkle with Parmesan cheese.

Jodi says: Serve this roast with a salad and fresh Italian bread.

Favorite recipe from ***Jodi Castiglione, Chandler, AZ***

Slow-Cooked Swiss Steak

Makes 6 servings

¼ cup all-purpose flour
2 teaspoons dry mustard
½ teaspoon salt
¼ teaspoon paprika
¼ teaspoon ground red pepper
¼ teaspoon black pepper
2 tablespoons oil
2 pounds beef round steak, cut into bite-size pieces
5 cups thinly sliced carrots
2 cups sliced onions
1 can (about 14 ounces) whole tomatoes, undrained
1 cup beef broth
1 tablespoon brown sugar
1 tablespoon honey
1 tablespoon Worcestershire sauce

1. Combine flour, mustard, salt, paprika, ground red pepper and black pepper in shallow bowl. Heat oil in large skillet over medium-high heat until hot. Dredge steak in flour mixture. Add steak to skillet; cook and stir until brown on all sides.

2. Transfer steak to slow cooker. Add remaining ingredients. Cover; cook on HIGH 4 to 5 hours or on LOW 7 to 9 hours.

Favorite recipe from ***Donna I. Abramchuk, Porterville, CA***

Best-Ever Roast

Makes 6 to 8 servings

1 beef chuck shoulder roast (3 to 5 pounds)
1 can (10¾ ounces) condensed cream of mushroom soup, undiluted
1 package (1 ounce) dry onion soup mix
4 to 5 medium potatoes, quartered
4 cups baby carrots

1. Place roast in slow cooker. (If necessary, cut roast in half to fit in slow cooker.) Add soup and soup mix. Cover; cook on LOW 2 hours.

2. Add potatoes and carrots. Cover; cook on LOW 4 hours or until potatoes are fork-tender.

*Favorite recipe from **Karen Mahan, El Dorado, KS***

Slow Cooker Round Steak with Gravy

Makes 4 servings

1 beef top round steak (about 1 pound)
1 can (10¾ ounces) condensed cream of chicken or cream of mushroom soup, undiluted
½ cup water
1 package (1 ounce) dry onion soup mix

Combine all ingredients in slow cooker. Cover; cook on LOW 8 hours or on HIGH 6 hours.

*Favorite recipe from **Tawnya Hopkins, Lexington, NC***

Sloppy Sloppy Joes

Makes 20 to 25 servings

4 pounds ground beef
1 cup chopped onion
1 cup chopped green bell pepper
1 can (about 28 ounces) tomato sauce
2 cans (10¾ ounces each) condensed tomato soup, undiluted
1 cup packed brown sugar
¼ cup ketchup
3 tablespoons Worcestershire sauce
1 tablespoon dry mustard
1 tablespoon prepared yellow mustard
1½ teaspoons chili powder
1 teaspoon garlic powder

1. Cook beef in large skillet over medium-high heat until no longer pink, stirring to break up meat. Drain fat. Add onion and bell pepper; cook, stirring frequently, 5 to 10 minutes or until onion becomes translucent and mixture becomes fragrant.

2. Transfer meat mixture to slow cooker. Add remaining ingredients; stir well to combine.

3. Cover; cook on LOW 4 to 6 hours.

Favorite recipe from ***Debbie Kraus, Phoenix, AZ***

Sloppy Sloppy Joe

Slow Cooker BBQ Beef

Makes 6 to 8 servings

1 beef chuck shoulder roast (3 pounds)
1 cup water
2 beef bouillon cubes
1 can (15 ounces) tomato sauce
¼ cup brown sugar
¼ cup ketchup
¼ cup prepared yellow mustard
1 tablespoon minced onion
Dash Worcestershire sauce

1. Place roast, water and bouillon cubes in slow cooker. Cover; cook on LOW 8 to 10 hours or until beef is tender.

2. Remove meat from slow cooker; shred with fork.

3. Discard all but 1 cup cooking liquid. Add shredded meat and remaining ingredients to slow cooker; stir to combine. Cover; cook on LOW 3 to 4 hours or on HIGH 1½ to 2 hours.

Vernell says: This BBQ Beef makes a great sandwich when served on your favorite rolls.

Favorite recipe from ***Vernell Harris, Milwaukee, WI***

Four-Layer Delight

Makes 4 servings

1½ teaspoons salt
1½ teaspoons dried thyme leaves
¾ teaspoon black pepper
½ pound sliced bacon, cut into 1-inch pieces
1 beef round or chuck steak (about 2 pounds)
3 large russet potatoes, scrubbed and sliced
2 large onions, thinly sliced

1. Combine salt, thyme and pepper in small bowl; set aside.

2. Sprinkle bacon pieces over bottom of slow cooker. Place steak on top of bacon; sprinkle with half of seasoning mixture. Add potatoes and onions; sprinkle with remaining seasoning mixture. Cover; cook on LOW 8 hours.

Anne says: There should be plenty of liquid in the slow cooker, but you may need to add some water after several hours of cooking.

Favorite recipe from ***Anne Saeger, Goldsboro, NC***

Best-Ever Slow Cooker Pot Roast

Makes 8 servings

1 beef chuck shoulder roast (3 to 4 pounds)
1 can (10 ounces) prepared beef gravy
1 package (1 ounce) au jus gravy mix
½ package Italian salad dressing mix (½ ounce)
½ cup dry red wine
2 tablespoons all-purpose flour
½ cup cold water

1. Place roast in slow cooker. Combine gravy, au jus mix, salad dressing mix and wine in medium bowl. Pour mixture over meat. Cover; cook on LOW 8 to 10 hours.

2. Remove roast to plate; cover with foil to keep warm. Turn slow cooker to HIGH. Mix flour into water until smooth. Stir into juices in slow cooker. Cook 15 minutes or until thickened.

Favorite recipe from ***Ann Foster, Redlands, CA***

Corned Beef and Cabbage

Makes 6 servings

1 head cabbage (1½ pounds), washed and cut into 6 wedges
4 ounces baby carrots
1 corned beef brisket (3 pounds) with seasoning packet
1 quart (4 cups) water
⅓ cup prepared yellow mustard (optional)
⅓ cup honey (optional)

1. Place cabbage in slow cooker; top with carrots.

2. Place seasoning packet* on top of vegetables. Place corned beef, fat side up, over seasoning packet and vegetables. Add water. Cover; cook on LOW 10 hours.

3. Discard seasoning packet. Just before serving, combine mustard and honey in small bowl. Serve as dipping sauce, if desired.

**If seasoning packet is not perforated, poke several small holes with tip of paring knife.*

Roast Beef with Mushrooms and Vegetables

Makes 8 servings

1 tablespoon vegetable oil
1 boneless beef chuck shoulder roast (3 to 5 pounds)
6 medium potatoes, peeled and halved
1 bag (1 pound) baby carrots
1 medium onion, quartered
1 can (10¾ ounces) condensed cream of mushroom soup, undiluted
1 cup water
1 can (4 ounces) sliced mushrooms, drained

1. Heat oil in large skillet over medium heat until hot. Brown roast on all sides. Drain fat. Transfer roast to slow cooker. (If necessary, cut roast in half to fit in slow cooker.) Add potatoes, carrots and onion around roast.

2. Combine soup, water and mushrooms in medium bowl. Pour over roast. Cover; cook on LOW 6 to 8 hours.

Favorite recipe from ***N.L. Banks, Hemet, CA***

Corned Beef and Cabbage

Mom's Easy Sunday Roast

Makes 6 to 8 servings

1 can (10¾ ounces) condensed cream of mushroom soup, undiluted
1 can (10¾ ounces) condensed tomato soup, undiluted
1 can (10¾ ounces) condensed cream of celery soup, undiluted
1 can (about 8 ounces) sliced mushrooms, drained
1 package (1 ounce) dry onion soup mix
4 Idaho potatoes, peeled and quartered
1 bag (1 pound) baby carrots
1 beef chuck roast (about 3 pounds)

1. Combine soups, mushrooms and dry onion soup mix in large bowl; mix well.

2. Place potatoes and carrots in bottom of slow cooker. Place roast on top of vegetables. Pour soup mixture over meat. Cover; cook on LOW 5 to 6 hours or until meat and vegetables are tender.

Favorite recipe from ***Marcia Anklam, Sterling Heights, MI***

Slow Cooker Hamburger Casserole

Makes 4 to 6 servings

1½ pounds 95% lean ground beef
4 medium potatoes, thinly sliced
3 carrots, thinly sliced
1 can (15 ounces) green peas, drained
1 can (15 ounces) corn, drained
3 medium onions, chopped
Salt
Black pepper
1 can (10¾ ounces) condensed tomato soup, undiluted
1 soup can water

1. Heat large nonstick skillet over medium-high heat. Add ground beef; cook and stir until browned. Drain fat.

2. Meanwhile, layer vegetables in slow cooker in order listed, seasoning occasionally with salt and pepper. Add beef over top. Cover with tomato soup and water. Cover; cook on LOW 6 to 8 hours or on HIGH 3 to 4 hours.

Favorite recipe from ***Ramona Hook Wysong, Barlow, KY***

Italian Beef

Makes 8 servings

1 beef rump roast (3 to 5 pounds)
2 cups mild jardinière
1 can (14 ounces) beef broth

1. Place roast in slow cooker. Pour jardinière and broth over top. Cover; cook on LOW 10 hours.

2. Shred beef; serve with sauce on crusty Italian rolls.

Favorite recipe from ***Marion Pagliuco, Avondale, AZ***

Tender Chuck Roast with Vegetables

Makes 6 servings

1 boneless beef chuck shoulder roast (2½ to 3 pounds)
Salt
Garlic powder
Black pepper
6 large carrots, cut into pieces
3 ribs celery, cut into pieces
3 medium potatoes, peeled and quartered
1 large onion, cut into wedges
2 cans (14½ ounces each) beef broth with onions
1 cup dry red wine
⅓ cup cold water
2 tablespoons cornstarch

1. Place roast in slow cooker; season to taste with salt, garlic powder and pepper to taste.

2. Add vegetables to slow cooker; season with salt and pepper to taste.

3. Pour broth and wine over vegetables and beef. Cover top tightly with foil. Cover foil with lid; cook on LOW 8 to 10 hours.

4. Remove meat and vegetables to serving dish; keep warm. Combine water and cornstarch in small bowl: stir into juices in slow cooker. Cook on HIGH 15 minutes or until juices are thickened. Serve gravy with meat and vegetables.

Favorite recipe from ***Cyndi White, Shreveport, LA***

Italian Beef

pork favorites

Harvest Ham Supper

Makes 6 servings

6 carrots, sliced in half lengthwise
3 large sweet potatoes, sliced in half lengthwise
1 boneless ham (about 1½ pounds)
1 cup maple syrup

1. Place carrots and potatoes in bottom of slow cooker. Place ham on top of vegetables. Pour syrup over ham and vegetables.

2. Cover; cook on LOW 6 to 8 hours.

Carol says: Our farm was a unique generational experience and one of our Spring adventures was to make and sell maple syrup to help defray the cost of taxes. This crock pot recipe was one of our favorites.

Favorite recipe from ***Carol A. Stone, Waverly, TN***

Harvest Ham Supper

Company Slow Cooker Pork Chops

Makes 4 to 6 servings

2 cans (10¾ ounces each) condensed fat-free cream of mushroom soup, undiluted
½ cup fat-free (skim) milk
1 package (3 ounces) reduced-fat cream cheese, softened
¼ cup fat-free sour cream
2 tablespoons vegetable oil
4 to 6 pork loin chops, cut ¾ inch thick
Salt
Black pepper
1 jar (2½ ounces) sliced dried beef

1. Combine soup, milk, cream cheese and sour cream in medium bowl until smooth; set aside.

2. Heat oil in large skillet over medium-high heat; brown both sides of pork chops. Drain fat. Season to taste with salt and pepper.

3. Spray inside of slow cooker with nonstick cooking spray. Place half of pork chops in slow cooker. Top with 4 slices dried beef. Pour half of sauce mixture over top. Repeat with remaining chops, dried beef and sauce. Cover; cook on LOW 8 to 9 hours.

Serving Suggestion: Serve with mashed potatoes.

Favorite recipe from ***Kim Carroll, Hastings, MN***

Savory Slow Cooker Pork Roast

Makes 8 servings

1 boneless pork blade or sirloin roast (3 to 4 pounds)
Salt
Black pepper
2 tablespoons vegetable oil
1 medium onion, sliced into ¼-inch-thick rings
2 to 3 cloves of garlic, chopped
1 can (14½ ounces) chicken broth

1. Season pork with salt and pepper. Heat oil in large skillet over medium heat; brown roast on all sides.

2. Place onion slices on bottom of slow cooker; sprinkle with garlic. Place roast on top of onions. Pour chicken broth over roast. Cover; cook on LOW 10 hours or on HIGH 6 to 7 hours.

Favorite recipe from ***Sally Delashmitt, Chattanooga, TN***

Cantonese Pork

Makes 8 servings

2 pork tenderloins (about 2 pounds)
1 tablespoon vegetable oil
1 can (8 ounces) pineapple chunks in juice, undrained
1 can (8 ounces) tomato sauce
2 cans (4 ounces each) sliced mushrooms, drained
1 medium onion, thinly sliced
3 tablespoons brown sugar
2 tablespoons Worcestershire sauce
1½ teaspoons salt
1½ teaspoons white vinegar
Hot cooked rice

1. Cut tenderloins in half lengthwise, then crosswise into ¼-inch-thick slices.

2. Heat oil in large nonstick skillet over medium-high heat. Brown pork on all sides. Drain fat.

3. Place pork and remaining ingredients except rice in slow cooker. Cover; cook on HIGH 4 hours or on LOW 6 to 8 hours. Serve over rice.

Favorite recipe from ***Stacy Pineault, Mahwah, NJ***

Cantonese Pork

Country-Style Ribs

Makes 4 to 6 servings

4 to 6 bone-in country-style ribs (2 to 3 pounds), trimmed of fat
Salt
Black pepper
1½ cups chopped onion
1 bottle (20 to 24 ounces) ketchup
2 cups plus 2 tablespoons water, divided
1 jar (about 16 ounces) unsweetened applesauce
2 tablespoons brown sugar
½ teaspoon hot pepper sauce
1 tablespoon cornstarch

1. Heat large nonstick skillet over medium-high heat. Season ribs with salt and pepper. Add ribs to skillet 1 or 2 at a time; brown on both sides. Transfer ribs to large plate. Repeat with remaining ribs.

2. Add onion to skillet. Cook and stir in pan drippings over medium-high heat 5 minutes or until tender. Remove skillet from heat.

3. Meanwhile, combine ketchup, 2 cups water, applesauce, brown sugar and hot pepper sauce in slow cooker; stir well. Add cooked onions with pan drippings; stir to combine. Add ribs, cutting as necessary to fit into slow cooker.

4. Cover; cook on LOW or MEDIUM-LOW 6 to 8 hours or until meat is cooked through and very tender.

5. Transfer ribs to large plate. Skim fat from sauce in slow cooker, if necessary.

6. Combine cornstarch and remaining 2 tablespoons water in small bowl; stir well to make thick paste. Stir into sauce in slow cooker. Cook on HIGH 5 to 10 minutes or until sauce begins to thicken. Return ribs to slow cooker. Serve ribs with sauce.

Favorite recipe from ***Shirley McLear, Manistique, MI***

Slow-Cooked Pork Chops

Makes 6 servings

1 teaspoon vegetable oil
6 pork loin chops (about 1½ to 1¾ pounds)
1 can (10¾ ounces) condensed cream of mushroom soup, undiluted
1 can (10¾ ounces) condensed cream of celery soup, undiluted
1 tablespoon beef bouillon granules
Salt
Black pepper
Hot cooked rice or mashed potatoes (optional)

1. Heat oil in large skillet over medium-low heat. Brown pork on both sides. Drain fat. Transfer pork to slow cooker.

2. Combine all remaining ingredients in medium bowl; pour over pork. Cover; cook on LOW 6 hours or until pork is tender. Adjust seasonings to taste, if desired. Serve over rice or mashed potatoes, if desired.

Lisa says: This is good served with steamed broccoli.

Favorite recipe from ***Lisa Langston, Conroe, TX***

Glazed Pork Loin Chops

Makes 4 servings

1 bag (1 pound) baby carrots
4 boneless pork loin chops (about 1 pound)
1 jar (8 ounces) apricot preserves

1. Place carrots in bottom of slow cooker. Place pork on top of carrots; brush with preserves.

2. Cover; cook on HIGH 4 hours or on LOW 8 hours.

Pamela says: Serve with seasoned or cheese-flavored instant mashed potatoes.

Favorite recipe from ***Pamela DeWall, Muskegon, MI***

Glazed Pork Loin Chops

Succulent Pork Chops

Makes 6 servings

2 teaspoons olive oil
6 boneless pork chops, cut ½ inch thick (about 1½ pounds)
1 can (10¾ ounces) condensed cream of chicken soup, undiluted
1 can (10¾ ounces) condensed cream of mushroom soup, undiluted
1 can (8 ounces) sliced mushrooms, drained
1 cup milk
2 teaspoons minced garlic
Salt
Black pepper

1. Heat oil in large skillet over medium-low heat. Brown pork chops on both sides. Drain fat. Transfer pork chops to slow cooker.

2. Add remaining ingredients over top. Cover; cook on LOW 8 to 10 hours or on HIGH 5 to 7 hours. Adjust seasonings to taste, if desired.

Catherine says: I like to serve this over seasoned rice.

Favorite recipe from ***Catherine Johnston, Mobile, AL***

Slow-Cooked Pork & Sauerkraut

Makes 6 servings

2 jars (32 ounces each) sauerkraut, rinsed and drained
2½ cups water
3 tablespoons prepared brown mustard
1 package (1 ounce) dry onion soup mix
1 boneless pork blade or sirloin roast (about 3 pounds)

1. Combine sauerkraut, water, mustard and soup mix in slow cooker; mix well. Add pork to slow cooker.

2. Cover; cook on LOW 8 hours.

Favorite recipe from ***Lynne Shukait, Amherst, OH***

Easy Pork Chop Dinner

Makes 6 servings

1 large onion, thinly sliced
3 to 4 medium baking potatoes, sliced
6 pork chops
1 can (10¾ ounces) reduced-fat condensed cream of celery soup, undiluted
½ cup water or milk

1. Place onion in bottom of slow cooker. Top with potatoes. Place pork chops over potatoes.

2. Combine soup and water in small bowl; pour over chops. Cover; cook on LOW 6 to 8 hours.

Marie says: Serve with salad or vegetables for a delicious dinner.

Favorite recipe from ***Marie Kaysen, Mequon, WI***

Cheesy Pork and Potatoes

Makes 6 servings

½ pound ground pork, cooked and crumbled
½ cup finely crushed saltine crackers
⅓ cup barbecue sauce
1 egg
3 tablespoons margarine
1 tablespoon vegetable oil
4 medium potatoes, peeled and thinly sliced
1 medium onion, thinly sliced
1 cup grated mozzarella cheese
⅔ cup evaporated milk
1 teaspoon salt
¼ teaspoon paprika
⅛ teaspoon black pepper
Chopped fresh parsley

1. Combine pork, crackers, barbecue sauce and egg in large bowl; shape mixture into 6 patties.

2. Heat margarine and oil in medium skillet over medium heat. Cook and stir potatoes and onion until lightly browned. Drain. Transfer to slow cooker.

3. Combine cheese, milk, salt, paprika and pepper in small bowl. Pour into slow cooker. Layer pork patties on top. Cover; cook on LOW 3 to 5 hours or until potatoes are fork-tender and pork is cooked through. Garnish with parsley.

Cheesy Pork and Potatoes

poultry dinners

Angel Wings

Makes 2 servings

1 can (10¾ ounces) condensed tomato soup, undiluted
¾ cup water
¼ cup packed light brown sugar
2½ tablespoons balsamic vinegar
2 tablespoons chopped shallots
10 chicken wings

1. Combine soup, water, sugar, vinegar and shallots in slow cooker; mix well.

2. Add chicken wings; stir to coat with sauce. Cover; cook on LOW 5 to 6 hours or until cooked through and glazed with sauce.

Favorite recipe from ***Sheila C. Elgart, Alexandria, VA***

Angel Wings

Chicken Delicious

Makes 6 servings

6 boneless skinless chicken breasts (about 1½ pounds)
½ teaspoon salt
½ teaspoon celery salt
½ teaspoon black pepper
¼ teaspoon paprika
1 can (10¾ ounces) condensed cream of mushroom soup, undiluted
1 can (10¾ ounces) condensed cream of celery soup, undiluted
⅓ cup dry sherry or white wine
½ cup grated Parmesan cheese

Season chicken with salt, celery salt, pepper and paprika; place in slow cooker. Combine soups and sherry in medium bowl; mix well. Pour over chicken. Sprinkle cheese over top. Cover; cook on LOW 8 to 10 hours.

Favorite recipe from ***Richard White, Lewistown, PA***

Chicken Reuben

Makes 4 to 6 servings

1 tablespoon butter or margarine
2 large sweet onions (preferably Vidalia), chopped
4 to 6 chicken breasts
1 jar (28 ounces) sauerkraut, drained
4 to 6 slices Swiss cheese
1 bottle (16 ounces) Thousand Island salad dressing

1. Heat butter in large skillet over medium-low heat. Add onion; cook and stir 5 minutes or until tender.

2. Place half of chicken breasts in slow cooker. Top with half of onion mixture, half of sauerkraut, half of cheese slices and half of salad dressing. Repeat layers. Cover; cook on LOW 6 to 8 hours.

Christine says: This recipe is outstanding. You're going to love it.

Favorite recipe from ***Christine Haney, Valley View, OH***

Chicken Slow Cooker

Makes 6 servings

3 pounds boneless skinless chicken breasts, cut into bite-size pieces
½ teaspoon salt
½ teaspoon black pepper
½ cup all-purpose flour
1 cup chopped onion
1 cup water
1 cup ketchup
½ cup chopped celery
½ cup chopped green bell pepper
2 tablespoons brown sugar
2 tablespoons Worcestershire sauce
2 cloves garlic, minced
1 bay leaf

1. Season chicken with salt and black pepper. Dust with flour.

2. Combine chicken and all remaining ingredients in slow cooker. Cover; cook on LOW 8 hours. Remove and discard bay leaf.

Donna says: Serve over rice or noodles.

Favorite recipe from ***Donna Sadler, Topsha, ME***

Slow Cooker Chicken and Dressing

Makes 4 servings

4 boneless skinless chicken breasts (about 1 pound)
Salt
Black pepper
4 slices (4 ounces) Swiss cheese
1 can (14½ ounces) chicken broth
2 cans (10¾ ounces each) condensed cream of chicken, celery or mushroom soup, undiluted
3 cups uncooked packaged stuffing mix
½ cup butter, melted

1. Place chicken in slow cooker. Season to taste with salt and pepper.

2. Top each breast with cheese slice. Add broth and soup. Sprinkle stuffing mix over top; pour melted butter over all. Cover; cook on LOW 6 to 8 hours or on HIGH 3 to 4 hours.

Shannon says: This is one of our favorites!

Favorite recipe from ***Shannon Athey, Bryn Mawr, PA***

Cream Cheese Chicken with Broccoli

Makes 8 servings

4 pounds boneless skinless chicken breasts, cut into ½-inch pieces
1 tablespoon olive oil
1 package (1 ounce) Italian salad dressing mix
Nonstick cooking spray
2 cups sliced mushrooms
1 cup chopped onion
1 can (10¾ ounces) condensed low-fat cream of chicken soup, undiluted
1 bag (10 ounces) frozen broccoli florets
1 package (8 ounces) reduced-fat cream cheese, cubed
¼ cup dry sherry

1. Toss chicken with olive oil. Sprinkle with Italian salad dressing mix. Place in slow cooker. Cover; cook on LOW 3 hours.

2. Spray large skillet with cooking spray. Add mushrooms and onion; cook 5 minutes over medium heat or until onions are tender, stirring occasionally.

3. Add soup, broccoli, cream cheese and sherry to skillet; cook and stir until hot. Transfer to slow cooker. Cover; cook on LOW 1 hour.

Favorite recipe from ***Pamela Wagner, Gainesville, FL***

Slow Cooker Chicken Mozambique

Makes 4 servings

2½ pounds skinless chicken breasts
1 cup dry white wine
½ cup (1 stick) margarine
1 small onion, chopped
2 tablespoons minced garlic
2 tablespoons lemon juice
2 tablespoons hot pepper sauce
1 teaspoon salt
3 to 4 cups hot cooked rice

Place all ingredients except rice in slow cooker. Cover; cook on LOW 8 hours or on HIGH 6 hours. Serve over rice.

Favorite recipe from ***Dorothy Marques, Fall River, MA***

Easy Chicken Alfredo

Makes 6 servings

1½ pounds chicken breasts, cut into ½-inch pieces
1 medium onion, chopped
1 tablespoon dried chives
1 tablespoon dried basil leaves
1 tablespoon extra-virgin olive oil
1 teaspoon lemon pepper
¼ teaspoon ground ginger
½ pound broccoli, coarsely chopped
1 red bell pepper, chopped
1 can (8 ounces) sliced water chestnuts, drained
1 cup baby carrots
3 cloves garlic, minced
1 jar (16 ounces) Alfredo sauce
1 package (8 ounces) wide egg noodles, cooked and drained

1. Combine chicken, onion, chives, basil, olive oil, lemon pepper and ginger in slow cooker; stir thoroughly. Add broccoli, bell pepper, water chestnuts, carrots and garlic. Mix well.

2. Cover; cook on LOW 8 hours or on HIGH 3 hours.

3. Add Alfredo sauce; stir to combine. Cover; cook 30 minutes or until heated through.

4. Serve over hot egg noodles.

Favorite recipe from ***Dorinda Ritter, Junction City, KS***

Easy Chicken Alfredo

Chicken in Honey Sauce

Makes 4 to 6 servings

4 to 6 boneless skinless chicken breasts (about 1 to 1½ pounds)
Salt
Black pepper
2 cups honey
1 cup soy sauce
½ cup ketchup
¼ cup vegetable oil
2 cloves garlic, minced
Sesame seeds

1. Place chicken in slow cooker; season with salt and pepper.

2. Combine honey, soy sauce, ketchup, oil and garlic in medium bowl. Pour over chicken. Cover; cook on LOW 6 to 8 hours or on HIGH 3 to 4 hours.

3. Garnish with sesame seeds before serving.

Favorite recipe from ***Carol Wright, Cartersville, GA***

Slow Cooker Chicken Dinner

Makes 4 servings

4 boneless skinless chicken breasts (about 1 pound)
1 can (10¾ ounces) condensed cream of chicken soup, undiluted
⅓ cup milk
1 package (6 ounces) unprepared stuffing mix
1⅔ cups water

1. Place chicken in slow cooker. Combine soup and milk in small bowl; mix well. Pour soup mixture over chicken.

2. Combine stuffing mix and water in medium bowl. Spoon stuffing over chicken. Cover; cook on LOW 6 to 8 hours.

Favorite recipe from ***Joanna Delaney, Chunchula, AL***

Kat's Slow Chicken

Makes 4 servings

1 cut-up whole chicken (3 pounds)
1 jar (26 ounces) spaghetti sauce
2 medium potatoes, cubed
1 medium green bell pepper, cut into strips
1 medium onion, sliced
1 carrot, sliced
1 rib celery, sliced
½ cup water
4 cloves garlic, minced

Combine all ingredients in slow cooker. Cover; cook on LOW 6 to 8 hours.

Kat says: When you come home, the house will smell good, dinner will be ready—and there's only one pot to clean!

Favorite recipe from ***Kat Sadi, San Luis Obispo, CA***

Chicken Parisienne

Makes 6 servings

1½ pounds boneless skinless chicken breasts, cubed
½ teaspoon salt
½ teaspoon paprika
½ teaspoon black pepper
1 can (10¾ ounces) condensed cream of mushroom or cream of chicken soup, undiluted
2 cans (4 ounces each) sliced mushrooms, drained
½ cup dry white wine
1 cup sour cream
6 cups hot cooked egg noodles

1. Place chicken in slow cooker. Sprinkle with salt, paprika and pepper.

2. Add soup, mushrooms and wine to slow cooker; mix well. Cover; cook on HIGH 2 to 3 hours. Add sour cream during last 30 minutes of cooking.

3. Serve chicken mixture over noodles. Garnish as desired.

Maureen says: For a taste-pleasing variation, try this dish over rice instead of noodles.

Favorite recipe from ***Maureen Baisden, Columbus, OH***

Chicken Parisienne

soups & stews

Nancy's Chicken-Noodle Soup

Makes 4 servings

1 large can (48 ounces) chicken broth
4 cups water
2 boneless skinless chicken breasts, cut into bite-size pieces
⅔ cup diced onion
⅔ cup diced celery
⅔ cup diced carrots
⅔ cup sliced mushrooms
½ cup frozen peas
4 chicken bouillon cubes
2 tablespoons margarine
1 tablespoon parsley flakes
1 teaspoon salt
1 teaspoon ground cumin
1 teaspoon dried marjoram leaves
1 teaspoon black pepper
2 cups hot cooked egg noodles

1. Combine all ingredients except noodles in slow cooker.

2. Cover; cook on LOW 4 to 6 hours or on HIGH 3 to 4 hours. Add noodles during last half hour of cooking.

Favorite recipe from ***Nancy Huck, Moses Lake, WA***

Nancy's Chicken-Noodle Soup

Roasted Tomato-Basil Soup

Makes 6 servings

2 cans (28 ounces each) peeled whole tomatoes, seeded and liquid reserved
2½ tablespoons packed dark brown sugar
1 medium onion, finely chopped
3 cups chicken broth
3 tablespoons tomato paste
¼ teaspoon ground allspice
1 can (5 ounces) evaporated milk
¼ cup shredded fresh basil leaves (about 10 large)
Salt
Black pepper

1. To roast tomatoes, preheat oven to 450°F. Line cookie sheet with foil; spray with nonstick cooking spray. Arrange tomatoes on foil in single layer. Sprinkle with brown sugar and top with onion. Bake about 25 to 30 minutes or until tomatoes look dry and light brown. Remove from oven. Let tomatoes cool slightly. Finely chop.

2. Place tomato mixture, 3 cups reserved liquid from tomatoes, chicken broth, tomato paste and allspice in slow cooker; mix well. Cover; cook on LOW 8 hours or on HIGH 4 hours.

3. Add evaporated milk and basil; season to taste with salt and pepper. Cook 30 minutes or until hot. Garnish as desired.

Roasted Tomato-Basil Soup

My Mother's Sausage & Vegetable Soup

Makes 6 to 8 servings

2 cups diced potatoes
1 can (15 ounces) black beans, rinsed and drained
1 can (14½ ounces) diced tomatoes, undrained
1 can (10¾ ounces) condensed cream of mushroom soup, undiluted
½ pound turkey sausage, cut into ½-inch slices
1 cup chopped onions
1 cup chopped red bell pepper
½ cup water
2 teaspoons extra-hot pepared horseradish
2 teaspoons honey
1 teaspoon dried basil leaves

Combine all ingredients in slow cooker; mix well. Cover; cook on LOW 7 to 8 hours or until potato is tender.

Favorite recipe from ***Margaret Pache, Mesa, AZ***

Harvest Beef Stew

Makes 6 servings

1 tablespoon olive oil
1½ pounds beef for stew
4 cups canned stewed tomatoes
6 carrots, cut into 1-inch pieces
3 medium potatoes, cut into 1-inch pieces
3 ribs celery, chopped (about 1 cup)
1 medium onion, sliced
1 cup apple juice
2 tablespoons dried parsley flakes
1 tablespoon dried basil leaves
2 teaspoons salt
1 clove garlic, minced
½ teaspoon black pepper
2 bay leaves
½ cup warm water (optional)
¼ cup all-purpose flour (optional)

1. Heat oil in large skillet over medium-low heat. Brown stew meat on all sides. Drain fat. Transfer meat to slow cooker.

2. Add all remaining ingredients except warm water and flour to slow cooker; mix well. Cover; cook on HIGH 6 to 7 hours.

3. Before serving, thicken gravy, if desired. Combine warm water and flour in small bowl, stirring well until all lumps are gone. Add mixture to liquid in slow cooker; mix well. Cook 10 to 20 minutes or until sauce thickens. Remove and discard bay leaves before serving.

Favorite recipe from ***Sue Szumski, Marseilles, IL***

Simple Hamburger Soup

Makes 8 servings

2 pounds ground beef or turkey, cooked and drained
1 can (28 ounces) whole tomatoes, undrained
2 cans (14 ounces each) beef broth
1 bag (10 ounces) frozen gumbo soup vegetables
½ cup uncooked pearl barley
1 teaspoon salt
1 teaspoon dried thyme leaves
Black pepper
Water

Combine all ingredients in slow cooker. Add water to cover. Cover; cook on HIGH 3 to 4 hours or until barley and vegetables are tender.

Gregg says: This soup is very easy to make. Try adding other frozen or canned vegetables or diced potatoes and carrots. Canned diced or stewed tomatoes can be substituted for the whole tomatoes. For a large crowd, add corn and serve with cornbread.

Favorite recipe from ***Gregg Sunderlin, Blairsville, PA***

Navy Bean & Ham Soup

Makes 6 servings.

1 pound cooked ham, cubed
6 cups water
5 cups navy beans, soaked overnight and drained
1 can (15 ounces) corn, drained
1 can (4 ounces) green chilies, drained and diced
1 onion, diced (optional)
Salt
Black pepper

Place all ingredients in slow cooker. Cover; cook on LOW 8 to 10 hours or until beans are tender. Serve with biscuits, if desired.

Favorite recipe from ***Jamey Goff, Bellevue, NE***

Slow Cooker Stew

Makes 4 to 6 servings

1 pound beef for stew
1 pound potatoes, peeled and diced
½ pound carrots, peeled and cut into 2-inch pieces *or* ½ pound baby carrots
2 medium onions, chopped
2 cans (15 ounces each) beef broth
1 envelope (1 ounce) au jus gravy mix
Water
1 bag (16 ounces) frozen peas
1 tablespoon cornstarch
2 tablespoons cold water

1. Place stew meat in slow cooker. Add potatoes, carrots, onions, broth, au jus mix and enough water to cover. Cover; cook on LOW 8 hours. Add frozen peas during last hour of cooking.

2. Just before serving, combine cornstarch and water in small bowl; stir into slow cooker juices. Cook 5 minutes or until sauce is thickened.

Jill says: You can substitute a cut-up chicken for the stew meat and add chicken broth instead of beef broth. Omit the au jus mix for a nice chicken stew.

Favorite recipe from ***Jill Simmons, Emporium, PA***

Navy Bean & Ham Soup

Grandma Ruth's Minestrone

Makes 4 servings

1 pound ground beef
1 cup dried red beans
1 package (16 ounces) frozen mixed vegetables
2 cans (8 ounces each) tomato sauce
1 can (14 ounces) diced tomatoes, undrained
¼ head cabbage, shredded
1 cup chopped onions
1 cup chopped celery
½ cup chopped parsley
1 tablespoon dried basil leaves
1 tablespoon dried Italian seasoning
1 teaspoon salt
1 teaspoon black pepper
1 cup cooked macaroni

1. Combine ground beef and beans in slow cooker. Cover; cook on HIGH 2 hours.

2. Add all remaining ingredients except macaroni; stir to combine. Cover; cook on LOW 6 to 8 hours or until beans are tender.

3. Add macaroni to slow cooker; stir well. Cover; cook on HIGH 1 hour.

Favorite recipe from ***Jamie Mozingo, LaPine, OR***

Slow Cooker Beef Stew

Makes 6 servings

¼ cup all-purpose flour
1 teaspoon salt
½ teaspoon black pepper
1 beef round steak, cut into ¾-inch pieces (about 2 pounds)
2 tablespoons vegetable oil
1½ cups water
1 package (about 1 ounce) beef stew seasoning mix
4 medium potatoes, cut into ½-inch cubes
3 cups sliced carrots
½ cup chopped onion
1 can (14½ ounces) beef broth

1. Combine flour, salt and pepper in small bowl. Coat beef with seasoned flour. Heat oil in large skillet over medium-high heat. Brown beef in batches. Add water and seasoning mix; stir well.

2. Place potatoes, carrots and onion in slow cooker. Top with beef mixture. Add beef broth. Cover; cook on LOW 6 to 8 hours or until vegetables are fork-tender.

Favorite recipe from ***Kim Miller, Fenton, MI***

Slow Cooker Steak Soup

Makes 4 servings

1 pound ground beef
4 cups tomato-vegetable juice
2 cups diced celery
2 cups diced carrots
1 can (15 ounces) diced tomatoes, drained
1 package (12 ounces) frozen mixed vegetables
1 cup chopped onion
5 tablespoons granulated beef bouillon
1 cup (2 sticks) margarine or butter
1 cup all-purpose flour

1. Cook and stir ground beef in large skillet over medium heat until no longer pink. Drain fat. Transfer beef to slow cooker.

2. Add tomato-vegetable juice, celery, carrots, tomatoes, mixed vegetables, onion and bouillon to slow cooker; stir to combine. Cover; cook on LOW 8 to 10 hours.

3. Melt margarine in medium saucepan over medium heat. Whisk in flour; cook until bubbly. Add flour mixture to slow cooker; mix well. Cook 1 hour on HIGH, with lid slightly open, until soup thickens.

Sharon says: Serve with salad and hot bread.

Favorite recipe from ***Sharon Sessa, Gulf Breeze, FL***

Great Chili

Makes 6 servings

1½ pounds ground beef
1½ cups chopped onions
1 cup chopped green bell pepper
2 cloves garlic, minced
3 cans (15 ounces each) dark red kidney beans, rinsed and drained
2 cans (15 ounces each) tomato sauce
1 can (14½ ounces) diced tomatoes, undrained
2 to 3 teaspoons chili powder
1 to 2 teaspoons dry hot mustard powder
¾ teaspoon dried basil leaves
½ teaspoon black pepper
1 to 2 dried hot chili peppers (optional)

1. Cook and stir ground beef, onions, bell pepper and garlic in large skillet until meat is browned and onion is tender. Drain fat. Transfer beef mixture to slow cooker.

2. Add kidney beans, tomato sauce, tomatoes with juice, chili powder, mustard, basil, black pepper and chili peppers, if desired; mix well. Cover; cook on LOW 8 to 10 hours or on HIGH 4 to 5 hours.

Favorite recipe from ***Catherine Dauphinee, Allenstown, NH***

Best-Ever Chili

Makes 8 servings

1½ pounds ground beef
1 cup chopped onion
2 cans (15 ounces each) kidney beans, 1 cup juice reserved
1½ pounds Roma tomatoes, diced
1 can (15 ounces) tomato paste
3 to 6 tablespoons chili powder

1. Cook and stir beef and onion in large skillet over medium-high heat 10 minutes or until meat is no longer pink. Drain fat. Transfer beef mixture to slow cooker.

2. Add kidney beans with 1 cup reserved juice, tomatoes, tomato paste and chili powder to slow cooker; mix well. Cover; cook on LOW 10 to 12 hours or until tomatoes are soft.

Favorite recipe from ***Terry Lunday, Flagstaff, AZ***

Vegetable Beef Soup

Makes 8 servings

3 pounds beef for stew
3 medium potatoes, diced
3 medium onions, diced
4 ribs celery, sliced
4 carrots, sliced
4 beef bouillon cubes
2 teaspoons salt
1 teaspoon black pepper
1 can (28 ounces) vegetable juice cocktail
5 cups water
2 packages (10 ounces each) frozen mixed vegetables, thawed

1. Place all ingredients except frozen vegetables in slow cooker in order listed above. Cover; cook on LOW 8 to 10 hours or on HIGH 4 to 6 hours.

2. Add thawed frozen vegetables during last 2 hours of cooking.

Favorite recipe from ***Priscilla Christian, Centerville, IN***

Quick-n-Easy Chili

Makes 4 servings

1 teaspoon vegetable oil
1 pound 95% lean ground beef
1 medium onion, chopped
1 package (1 ounce) chili seasoning mix
1 can (46 ounces) tomato juice
1 large can (28 ounces) diced tomatoes, undrained
1 can (15 ounces) light red kidney beans, rinsed and drained
1 can (4 ounces) sliced mushrooms, drained

1. Heat oil in large skillet over medium-low heat. Add beef and onion; cook and stir until beef is browned. Drain fat.

2. Place beef mixture in slow cooker. Add chili seasoning mix; stir. Add tomato juice, tomatoes, kidney beans and mushrooms; mix well. Cover; cook on HIGH 1 to 2 hours or until all ingredients are heated through. Reduce heat to LOW; cook 6 to 8 hours.

Favorite recipe from ***Wilma Hill, Pt. Pleasant, WV***

Creamy Slow Cooker Seafood Chowder

Makes 8 to 10 servings

1 quart (4 cups) half-and-half
2 cans (14½ ounces each) whole white potatoes, drained and cubed
1 bag (16 ounces) frozen hash brown potatoes
2 cans (10¾ ounces) condensed cream of mushroom soup, undiluted
1 onion, minced
½ cup (1 stick) butter, cut into pieces
1 teaspoon salt
1 teaspoon black pepper
5 cans (about 8 ounces each) whole oysters, rinsed and drained
2 cans (about 6 ounces each) minced clams, undrained
2 cans (about 4 ounces each) cocktail shrimp, rinsed and drained

1. Combine half-and-half, canned and frozen potatoes, soup, onion, butter, salt and pepper in slow cooker; mix thoroughly.

2. Add oysters, clams and shrimp; stir gently.

3. Cover; cook on LOW 4 to 5 hours. Garnish as desired.

Carl says: I make this easy chowder in a 6½-quart slow cooker. It serves 8 to 10 people as a main course. Along with grilled cheese sandwiches, it's become our traditional Christmas Eve meal. It would be good for a football get-together on a cold winter's afternoon, too.

Favorite recipe from ***Carl E. Parry, Olathe, KS***

Creamy Slow Cooker Seafood Chowder

Slow and Easy Chili con Carne

Makes 8 servings

1 tablespoon vegetable oil
1 cup chopped onion
3 large cloves garlic, crushed
2 pounds ground beef
1 can (28 ounces) pinto beans, rinsed and drained
1 can (28 ounces) chopped tomatoes, undrained
¼ cup hot sauce
2 teaspoons salt
2 teaspoons dried oregano leaves
2 teaspoons ground cumin
½ teaspoon black pepper

1. Heat oil in large skillet over medium-high heat. Add onion and garlic; cook and stir until onion is tender. Add beef; cook and stir until beef is no longer pink. Drain fat. Transfer beef mixture to slow cooker.

2. Add beans, tomatoes, hot sauce, salt, oregano, cumin and pepper to slow cooker; stir to combine. Cover; cook on LOW 4 to 6 hours.

Laura says: Serve this dish with warm tortillas!

Favorite recipe from ***Laura Ivy Moore, Oxnard, CA***

Posole

Makes 8 servings

3 pounds boneless pork, cubed
3 cans (14 ounces each) white hominy, drained
¾ cup chili sauce

1. Combine all ingredients in slow cooker.

2. Cover; cook on HIGH 5 hours. Reduce temperature to LOW; cook additional 10 hours.

Favorite recipe from ***Billie Olofson, Des Moines, IA***

Potato-Cheddar Soup

Makes 6 servings

2 pounds red-skin potatoes, peeled and cut into ½-inch cubes
3 cups chicken broth
¾ cup coarsely chopped carrots
1 medium onion, coarsely chopped
½ teaspoon salt
1 cup half-and-half
¼ teaspoon black pepper
2 cups (8 ounces) shredded Cheddar cheese

1. Place potatoes, broth, carrots, onion and salt in slow cooker. Cover; cook on LOW 6 to 7 hours or on HIGH 3 to 3½ hours or until vegetables are tender.

2. Stir in half-and-half and pepper. Cover; cook on HIGH 15 minutes. Turn off heat and remove cover; let stand 5 minutes. Stir in cheese until melted.

Susan says: I like to serve this soup topped with whole wheat croutons.

Favorite recipe from ***Susan Richardson, Libertyville, IL***

Seafood Gumbo

Makes 6 to 8 servings

2 tablespoons vegetable oil
1 green bell pepper, chopped
1 large onion, chopped
2 cloves garlic, minced
3 cans (10¾ ounces each) condensed golden mushroom soup, undiluted
1 jar (24 ounces) mild or medium Southwest salsa with beans and corn
2 pounds frozen seafood blend, thawed

1. Heat oil in medium saucepan. Add bell pepper, onion and garlic. Cook and stir over medium-high heat about 3 to 4 minutes or until tender. Transfer to slow cooker.

2. Add soup and salsa to slow cooker. Cover; cook on LOW 3 hours. Add seafood during last hour of cooking.

Simone says: Serve with steamed wild rice or harvest bread.

Favorite recipe from ***Simone Sprague, Carmel, CA***

world fare

Mexican Meat Loaf

Makes 4 to 6 servings

2 pounds ground beef
2 cups crushed corn chips
1 cup shredded Cheddar cheese
⅔ cup salsa
2 eggs, beaten
4 tablespoons taco seasoning

1. Combine all ingredients in large bowl; mix well.

2. Shape mixture into loaf; place in slow cooker. Cover; cook on LOW 8 to 10 hours.

Nancy says: This meat loaf is easy and moist.

Tip: For a glaze, combine ½ cup ketchup, 2 tablespoons brown sugar and 1 teaspoon dry mustard in small bowl. Spread over cooked meat loaf. Cover; cook on HIGH 15 minutes.

Favorite recipe from ***Nancy Crew, Napoleon, OH***

Mexican Meat Loaf

Simple Shredded Pork Tacos

Makes 6 servings

2 pounds boneless pork roast
1 cup salsa
1 can (4 ounces) chopped mild green chilies
½ teaspoon garlic salt
½ teaspoon black pepper
Tortillas, warmed

1. Place all ingredients in slow cooker. Cover; cook on MEDIUM 8 hours or until meat is tender.

2. Use 2 forks to shred pork before serving.

Rose says: Serve this pork with tortillas and your favorite condiments.

Favorite recipe from ***Rose Hooper, Jamul, CA***

Chicken Italiano

Makes 4 servings

1 chicken (5 pounds), quartered
1 cup water
1 can (8 ounces) tomato sauce
1 package (6¼ ounces) spaghetti sauce seasoning mix
1 can (8 ounces) sliced mushrooms, drained
1 teaspoon dried Italian seasoning

1. Place chicken in slow cooker. Combine water, tomato sauce and seasoning mix in small bowl; mix well. Pour over chicken.

2. Place mushrooms on top of sauce. Sprinkle with Italian seasoning. Cover; cook on LOW 4 hours.

Favorite recipe from ***Mary Lou Strunk, Salem, IL***

Simple Shredded Pork Tacos

Russian Pot Roast

Makes 10 to 12 servings

1 tablespoon olive oil
1 medium onion, chopped
3 pounds boneless beef chuck shoulder roast
Salt
Black pepper
1 large potato, cut into ½-inch cubes
2 large carrots, sliced into ¼-inch-thick pieces
½ cup dried lima beans
½ cup dried kidney beans
½ cup dried pinto beans
½ cup dried lentils
½ cup uncooked pearl barley
1 clove garlic, minced
½ cup ketchup or tomato sauce

1. Heat oil in large skillet over medium-high heat. Add onion; cook, stirring frequently, until tender.

2. Season roast with salt and pepper to taste. Add to skillet with onion. Brown on all sides. Transfer roast and onion to slow cooker.

3. Add remaining ingredients except ketchup to slow cooker. Spread ketchup over top of roast. Add enough water to cover all. Cover; cook on HIGH 10 hours or until meat is tender and falling apart.

Favorite recipe from ***Margie Herman, Mill Valley, CA***

German Kraut and Sausage

Makes 8 servings

5 medium potatoes, cut into ½-inch cubes
1 large onion, cut into ¼-inch-thick slices
½ medium green bell pepper, chopped
1 jar (32 ounces) sauerkraut, undrained
3 pounds kielbasa sausage, cut into 1-inch pieces
¼ cup packed brown sugar
1 teaspoon garlic powder
½ teaspoon black pepper

1. Place potatoes in slow cooker. Layer onion, bell pepper and sauerkraut over top.

2. Brown sausage in large skillet over medium-high heat. Transfer to slow cooker.

3. Combine brown sugar, garlic powder and black pepper in small bowl. Sprinkle over sausage.

4. Cover; cook on LOW 8 hours or until potatoes are fork-tender.

Favorite recipe from ***Leann Miller, Woodhaven, MI***

Greek-Style Chicken

Makes 4 to 6 servings

6 boneless skinless chicken thighs, trimmed of visible fat
½ teaspoon salt
½ teaspoon black pepper
1 tablespoon olive oil
½ cup chicken broth
1 lemon, thinly sliced
¼ cup pitted kalamata olives
½ teaspoon dried oregano leaves
1 clove garlic, minced
Hot cooked orzo or rice

1. Season chicken with salt and pepper. Heat oil in large skillet over medium-high heat. Brown chicken on all sides. Transfer to slow cooker.

2. Add broth, lemon, olives, oregano and garlic to slow cooker. Cover; cook on LOW 5 to 6 hours or until chicken is tender. Serve with orzo.

Prep Time: 15 minutes
Cook Time: 5 to 6 hours

Greek-Style Chicken

Ollie Green Chili Burro Enchilada-Style

Makes 6 servings

2 tablespoons vegetable oil
2 pounds pork, cut into cubes
Salt
Black pepper
¼ cup all-purpose flour
1 can (16 ounces) enchilada sauce
2 cans (7 ounces each) diced mild green chilies, drained
1 can (10¾ ounces) condensed cream of mushroom soup, undiluted
1 medium onion, chopped
1 can (2¼ ounces) sliced olives, drained
1 teaspoon ground cumin
½ teaspoon garlic powder
12 (8-inch) corn tortillas
4 cups (16 ounces) shredded Monterrey Jack cheese, divided

1. Heat oil in large skillet over medium-high heat. Season pork with salt and pepper. Lightly dust with flour. Add pork to skillet; cook and stir until browned and no longer pink in center.

2. Combine pork, enchilada sauce, chilies, soup, onion, olives, cumin and garlic powder in large bowl; mix well.

3. Reserve 1 cup cheese. Place ¼ of pork mixture in bottom of slow cooker. Top with 3 to 4 tortillas (torn to fit) and 1 cup remaining cheese. Repeat layers twice, ending with meat.

4. Cover; cook on LOW 3½ hours. Top with reserved 1 cup cheese. Cover; cook on LOW 30 minutes.

Favorite recipe from ***Cynthia Nash, Glendale, AZ***

Beef and Cabbage à la Mexicana

Makes 6 servings

1 head cabbage, separated into individual leaves
1 box (about 10 ounces) Spanish-style rice mix, plus ingredients to prepare
2 pounds ground beef
1 cup Italian-style bread crumbs
1 cup chopped onion
1 cup chopped green bell pepper
2 eggs, beaten
1 tablespoon Worcestershire sauce
1 teaspoon taco seasoning
1 clove garlic, minced
Salt
Black pepper
1 bottle (about 32 ounces) tomato juice

1. Bring 3 cups water to a boil in large saucepan. Add cabbage leaves; cook 3 minutes or until tender. Remove leaves with slotted spoon; drain. Set aside.

2. Prepare Spanish rice according to package directions; set aside.

3. Combine ground beef, bread crumbs, onion, bell pepper, eggs, Worcestershire sauce, taco seasoning and garlic in large bowl. Season with salt and black pepper.

4. Place 1 cabbage leaf on plate. Top with ½ cup beef mixture and ¼ cup Spanish rice. Roll up leaf; secure with wooden pick. Place, seam side down, in slow cooker. Repeat with remaining cabbage leaves, beef mixture and rice. Pour tomato juice over cabbage rolls. Cover; cook on HIGH 4 to 6 hours.

Favorite recipe from ***Charlotte Taylor, Midway, WV***

Italian Chicken with Sausage and Peppers

Makes 6 servings

2½ pounds chicken pieces
2 tablespoons olive oil
½ to ¾ pound sweet Italian sausage
2 green bell peppers, chopped
1 medium onion, chopped
1 carrot, finely chopped
2 cloves garlic, minced
1 can (19 ounces) tomato soup
1 can (15 ounces) tomato sauce
¼ teaspoon dried oregano leaves
¼ teaspoon dried basil leaves
1 bay leaf
Salt
Black pepper

1. Rinse chicken; pat dry. Heat oil in large skillet over medium-high heat. Add chicken, skin side down. Cook about 10 minutes or until browned on both sides. Remove from skillet; set aside.

2. Add sausage to skillet; cook 4 to 5 minutes or until browned. Remove from skillet. Cut into 1-inch pieces; set aside. Drain fat from skillet, reserving 1 tablespoon.

3. Add bell peppers, onion, carrot and garlic to skillet. Cook and stir 4 to 5 minutes or until vegetables are tender.

4. Add tomato soup, tomato sauce, oregano, basil and bay leaf to skillet with vegetables; stir well. Season to taste with salt and black pepper. Transfer mixture to slow cooker.

5. Add chicken and sausage to slow cooker. Cover; cook on LOW 6 to 8 hours or on HIGH 4 to 6 hours. Remove and discard bay leaf.

Favorite recipe from ***Dolores Hunter, West Homestead, PA***

Italian Chicken with Sausage and Peppers

Easy Parmesan Chicken

Makes 4 servings

8 ounces mushrooms, sliced
1 medium onion, cut into thin wedges
1 tablespoon olive oil
4 boneless skinless chicken breasts (about 1 pound)
1 jar (26 ounces) spaghetti sauce
½ teaspoon dried basil leaves
¼ teaspoon dried oregano leaves
1 bay leaf
½ cup (2 ounces) shredded part-skim mozzarella cheese
¼ cup grated Parmesan cheese
Hot cooked spaghetti (optional)

1. Place mushrooms and onion in slow cooker.

2. Heat oil in large skillet over medium-high heat until hot. Lightly brown chicken on both sides. Transfer chicken to slow cooker. Pour spaghetti sauce over chicken. Add herbs. Cook on HIGH 3 hours or on LOW 6 to 7 hours or until chicken is no longer pink in center. Remove and discard bay leaf.

3. Sprinkle chicken with cheeses. Cook, uncovered, on LOW 15 to 30 minutes or until cheeses are melted. Serve over spaghetti, if desired.

Susan says: Other vegetables, such as sliced zucchini, cubed eggplant or broccoli florets, can be substituted for the mushroom slices.

Favorite recipe from ***Susan Richardson, Libertyville, IL***

Peking Pork Chops

Makes 6 servings

6 pork chops, cut about 1 inch thick, trimmed of fat
½ cup soy sauce or teriyaki sauce
¼ cup packed brown sugar
¼ cup Chinese ketchup or regular ketchup
1 teaspoon ground ginger
1 to 2 cloves garlic, crushed
Salt (optional)
Black pepper (optional)

1. Place chops in slow cooker.

2. Combine soy sauce, brown sugar, ketchup, ginger and garlic in small bowl; pour over meat. Cover; cook on LOW 4 to 6 hours or until pork is tender. Season to taste with salt and pepper, if desired.

Lynda says: Serve these chops with steamed white rice and crisp Chinese noodles. I prefer jasmine or sticky rice.

Favorite recipe from ***Lynda McCormick, Burkburnett, TX***

Fiesta Chicken Burritos

Makes 4 servings

1 pound boneless skinless chicken breasts, diced
1 jar (32 ounces) chunky salsa
1 green bell pepper, chopped
1 medium onion, chopped
Soft flour tortillas, warmed

Place all ingredients in slow cooker. Cover; cook on LOW 4 to 6 hours.

Jenifer says: Serve this chicken with tortillas, cheese and sour cream.

Favorite recipe from ***Jenifer Leiendecker, Escondido, CA***

Moroccan Chicken Tagine

Makes 4 to 6 servings

3 pounds skinless chicken pieces
2 cups chicken broth
1 can (14½ ounces) diced tomatoes, undrained
2 medium onions, chopped
1 cup dried apricots, chopped
4 cloves garlic, minced
2 teaspoons ground cumin
1 teaspoon ground cinnamon
1 teaspoon ground ginger
½ teaspoon ground coriander
½ teaspoon ground red pepper
6 sprigs fresh cilantro
1 tablespoon cornstarch
1 tablespoon water
1 can (15 ounces) chick-peas, rinsed and drained
¼ cup slivered almonds, toasted
2 tablespoons chopped fresh cilantro
Hot cooked couscous or rice

1. Place chicken in slow cooker. Combine broth, tomatoes with juice, onions, apricots, garlic, cumin, cinnamon, ginger, coriander, red pepper and cilantro sprigs in medium bowl; pour over chicken. Cover; cook on LOW 4 to 5 hours or until chicken is no longer pink in center. Transfer chicken to serving platter; cover to keep warm.

2. Combine cornstarch and water in small bowl; mix until smooth. Stir cornstarch mixture and chick-peas into slow cooker. Cover; cook on HIGH 15 minutes or until sauce is thickened. Pour sauce over chicken. Sprinkle with almonds and cilantro. Serve with couscous.

Tip: To toast almonds, heat small nonstick skillet over medium-high heat. Add almonds; cook and stir about 3 minutes or until golden brown. Remove from pan at once. Let cool before adding to other ingredients.

Moroccan Chicken Tagine

Italian-Style Country Pork Ribs

Makes 4 servings

2 tablespoons vegetable oil
2 pounds boneless pork loin country-style ribs*
1 jar (32 ounces) spaghetti sauce
1 pound pasta (any variety), cooked and drained
Grated Parmesan cheese

**Ask your butcher for this cut, or substitute boneless pork sirloin chops.*

1. Heat oil in large skillet over medium-high heat. Add ribs in small batches; cook about 9 to 10 minutes or until browned on both sides. Transfer ribs to slow cooker. Repeat with remaining ribs.

2. Add spaghetti sauce to slow cooker. Cover; cook on LOW 6 to 8 hours or until meat is tender.

3. Add pasta to slow cooker during last 10 minutes of cooking. Serve pasta and ribs with Parmesan cheese garnish.

Favorite recipe from ***Judith Granger, Curlew, WA***

Chicken Cacciatore

Makes 6 to 8 servings

¼ cup vegetable oil
2½ to 3 pounds chicken pieces
1 can (28 ounces) crushed Italian-style tomatoes
2 cans (8 ounces each) Italian-style tomato sauce
1 medium onion, chopped
1 can (4 ounces) sliced mushrooms, drained
2 cloves garlic, minced
1 teaspoon salt
1 teaspoon dried oregano leaves
½ teaspoon dried thyme leaves
½ teaspoon black pepper
Hot cooked spaghetti or rice

1. Heat oil in large skillet over medium-low heat. Brown chicken on all sides. Drain fat. Transfer chicken to slow cooker.

2. Add remaining ingredients except spaghetti to slow cooker. Cover; cook on LOW 6 to 8 hours. Serve chicken mixture over spaghetti.

Favorite recipe from ***Carmen Bryce, Lloydminster, Alberta, Canada***

MY FAVORITES

My Favorite Recipes

Favorite recipe: ______________________________

Favorite recipe from: ______________________________

Ingredients: ______________________________

____

____

____

____

____

Method: ______________________________

____

____

____

____

____

____

____

____

____

____

____

____

My Favorite Recipes

Favorite recipe: ______________________________

Favorite recipe from: ______________________________

Ingredients: ______________________________

____

____

____

____

____

Method: ______________________________

____

____

____

____

____

____

____

____

____

____

____

____

My Favorite Recipes

Favorite recipe: ______________________________

Favorite recipe from: ______________________________

Ingredients: ______________________________

____

____

____

____

____

Method: ______________________________

____

____

____

____

____

____

____

____

____

____

____

____

My Favorite Recipes

Favorite recipe: ______________________

Favorite recipe from: ______________________

Ingredients: ______________________

____

____

____

____

____

Method: ______________________

____

____

____

____

____

____

____

____

____

____

____

____

My Favorite Recipes

Favorite recipe: ______________________________

Favorite recipe from: ______________________________

Ingredients: ______________________________

____

____

____

____

____

Method: ______________________________

____

____

____

____

____

____

____

____

____

____

____

____

My Favorite Recipes

Favorite recipe: ____________________

Favorite recipe from: ____________________

Ingredients: ____________________

Method: ____________________

My Favorite Recipes

Favorite recipe: ______________________

Favorite recipe from: ______________________

Ingredients: ______________________

Method: ______________________

My Favorite Recipes

Favorite recipe: ______________________________

Favorite recipe from: ______________________________

Ingredients: ______________________________

____

____

____

____

____

Method: ______________________________

____

____

____

____

____

____

____

____

____

____

____

____

My Favorite Recipes

Favorite recipe: ______________________________

Favorite recipe from: ______________________________

Ingredients: ______________________________

____

____

____

____

____

Method: ______________________________

____

____

____

____

____

____

____

____

____

____

____

____

My Favorite Recipes

Favorite recipe: ______________________

Favorite recipe from: ______________________

Ingredients: ______________________

Method: ______________________

My Favorite Recipes

Favorite recipe: ______________________

Favorite recipe from: ______________________

Ingredients: ______________________

Method: ______________________

My Favorite Recipes

Favorite recipe: ______________________________

Favorite recipe from: ______________________________

Ingredients: ______________________________

Method: ______________________________

My Favorite Recipes

Favorite recipe: ______________________________

Favorite recipe from: ______________________________

Ingredients: ______________________________

____

____

____

____

____

Method: ______________________________

____

____

____

____

____

____

____

____

____

____

____

____

My Favorite Recipes

Favorite recipe: ______________________________

Favorite recipe from: ______________________________

Ingredients: ______________________________

____

____

____

____

____

Method: ______________________________

____

____

____

____

____

____

____

____

____

____

____

____

My Favorite Recipes

Favorite recipe: ______________________________

Favorite recipe from: ______________________________

Ingredients: ______________________________

Method: ______________________________

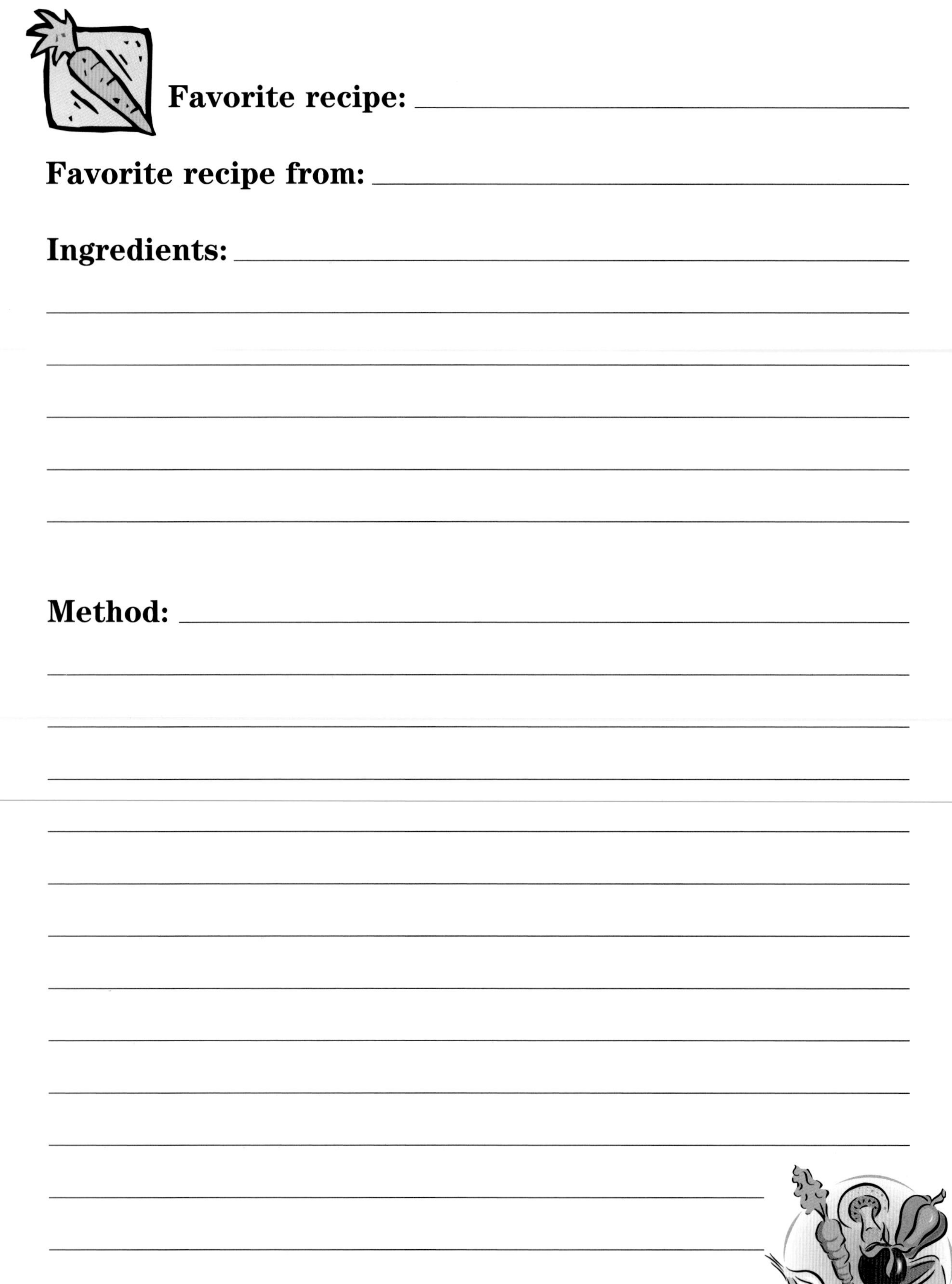

My Favorite Recipes

Favorite recipe: ______________________

Favorite recipe from: ______________________

Ingredients: ______________________

Method: ______________________

My Favorite Recipes

Favorite recipe: ______________________________

Favorite recipe from: ______________________________

Ingredients: ______________________________

Method: ______________________________

My Favorite Recipes

Favorite recipe: ______________________________

Favorite recipe from: ______________________________

Ingredients: ______________________________

____

____

____

____

____

Method: ______________________________

____

____

____

____

____

____

____

____

____

____

____

____

My Favorite Recipes

Favorite recipe: ______________________

Favorite recipe from: ______________________

Ingredients: ______________________

Method: ______________________

My Favorite Recipes

Favorite recipe: ____________________

Favorite recipe from: ____________________

Ingredients: ____________________

Method: ____________________

My Favorite Recipes

Favorite recipe: ______________________

Favorite recipe from: ______________________

Ingredients: ______________________

Method: ______________________

My Favorite Weeknight Meals

Favorite recipe: ______________________________

Favorite recipe from: ______________________________

____

Ingredients: ______________________________

____

____

____

____

Method: ______________________________

____

____

____

____

____

____

____

____

____

____

____

____

My Favorite Weeknight Meals

Favorite recipe: ______________________________

Favorite recipe from: ______________________________

____

Ingredients: ______________________________

____

____

____

____

Method: ______________________________

____

____

____

____

____

____

____

____

____

____

____

____

My Favorite Dinner Party

Occasion:

Guests:

Menu:

My Favorite Dinner Party

Date: ______________________________

Occasion: ______________________________

____

Guests: ______________________________

____

____

____

____

Menu: ______________________________

____

____

____

____

____

____

____

____

____

____

____

____

My Favorite Pot-Luck Recipes

Favorite recipe: ______________________________

Favorite recipe from: ______________________________

____

Ingredients: ______________________________

____

____

____

____

Method: ______________________________

____

____

____

____

____

____

____

____

____

____

____

____

My Favorite Pot-Luck Recipes

Favorite recipe: ________________

Favorite recipe from: ________________

____

Ingredients: ________________

____

____

____

____

Method: ________________

____

____

____

____

____

____

____

____

____

____

____

____

My Favorite Pot-Luck Recipes

Favorite recipe: ______________________________

Favorite recipe from: ______________________________

____

Ingredients: ______________________________

____

____

____

____

Method: ______________________________

____

____

____

____

____

____

____

____

____

____

____

____

My Favorite Pot-Luck Recipes

Favorite recipe: ______________________________________

Favorite recipe from: __________________________________

Ingredients: ____

Method: ____

My Favorite Pot-Luck Recipes

Favorite recipe: ______________________________

Favorite recipe from: ______________________________

____

Ingredients: ______________________________

____

____

____

____

Method: ______________________________

____

____

____

____

____

____

____

____

____

____

____

____

My Favorite Friends

Friend: ______________________________

Favorite foods: ______________________________

Don't serve: ______________________________

My Favorite Friends

Friend: ______________________________

Favorite foods: ______________________________

Don't serve: ______________________________

HINTS, TIPS & INDEX

The Basics

- Slow cookers were introduced in the 1970's and are finding renewed popularity today. There are two types of slow cookers. The most common models have heat coils circling the crockery insert, allowing heat to surround the food and cook evenly. The LOW (about 200°F) and HIGH (about 300°F) settings regulate cooking temperatures. One hour on HIGH equals 2 to 2½ hours on LOW. Less common slow cooker models have heat coils only on the bottom and have an adjustable thermostat. For this type, consult the manufacturer's instructions for advice on converting the recipes in this cookbook.
- As with conventional cooking recipes, slow cooker recipe time ranges are provided to account for variables such as temperature of ingredients before cooking, how full the slow cooker is and even altitude. Once you become familiar with your slow cooker you'll have a good idea which end of the range to use.
- Manufacturers recommend slow cookers be ½ to ¾ full for best results.
- Keep a lid on it! The slow cooker can take as long as twenty minutes to regain the heat lost when the cover is removed. If the recipe calls for stirring or checking the dish near the end of the cooking time, replace the lid as quickly as possible.
- Save money and gain flavor by choosing tougher, inexpensive cuts of meat. The long cooking times help tenderize the meat.
- Always taste the finished dish before serving and adjust seasonings to taste. Consider adding a dash of any of the following: salt, seasoned salt, freshly ground pepper, minced fresh herbs, seasoned herb blends, lemon juice, soy sauce, Worcestershire sauce or flavored vinegar.
- Follow the manufacturer's instructions for cleaning the slow cooker. To make cleanup even easier, spray the inside of the slow cooker with nonstick cooking spray before adding food.

The Benefits

- There is no need for constant attention or stirring.
- You never have to worry about burning or overcooking.
- Your sink will be free of pots or pans to scrub at the end of a long day.
- It is the perfect helper for parties and buffets.
- The kitchen stays cool, since the oven stays off.

- Even though the slow cooker is on for hours, it saves energy. On the LOW setting, it still uses less energy than most light bulbs.

TIPS & TECHNIQUES

Adapting Recipes

If you want to adapt a favorite recipe to a slow cooker method, follow these guidelines:

- Try to find a similar recipe in this publication or your manufacturer's guide. Note the cooking times, liquid amounts, ingredient quantities and sizes of meat and vegetable pieces.
- Because the slow cooker retains moisture, you will want to reduce the amount of liquid, often by as much as half.
- To prevent foods from curdling, add dairy products toward the end of cooking times.

Selecting the Right Meat

A good tip to keep in mind when shopping for meat is that you can, and in fact should, use tougher, inexpensive cuts of meat. Top-quality cuts such as loin chops and filet mignon tend to fall apart during long cooking times. Instead, plan to use these top-quality meats for roasting, broiling or grilling. Save money by using less expensive cuts for your slow cooker. You will be amazed to find even the toughest cuts of meat come out fork-tender and flavorful.

Reducing Fat

The slow cooker can help reduce fat in meals, simply because foods are not cooked in oil like they are when stir-fried and sautéed. Plus, tougher, less-expensive cuts of meat tend to have less fat than prime cuts. For fatty cuts, such as ribs, consider browning them first on top of the range to cook off excess fat.

Chicken skin tends to shrivel and curl in the slow cooker; therefore, most recipes call for skinless chicken. To remove the skin from chicken, use the following technique: Freeze the chicken until it is firm but not hard. (Do not freeze thawed chicken.) Grasp the chicken skin with a clean kitchen towel or paper towel and pull it away from the meat. After skinning the chicken, be sure to launder the towel before using it again (to prevent cross-contamination).

Most of the fat from accumulated juices, soups and canned broths can be easily removed. The simplest way is to refrigerate the liquid for several hours or overnight. The fat will float to the top and congeal for easy removal. If you plan to use the liquid right away, ladle it into a bowl or measuring cup. Let it stand about 5 minutes so the fat can rise to the surface. Skim the fat with a large spoon. You can also lightly pull a clean paper towel over the surface, allowing the grease to be absorbed. To degrease canned broth, refrigerate the unopened can. Simply spoon the congealed fat off the surface after opening the can.

Cutting Vegetables

Vegetables often take longer to cook than meats. Cut the vegetables into small, thin pieces and place them on the bottom or near the side of the slow cooker. Carefully follow recipe instructions, being sure to cut vegetables to the proper size.

Foil to the Rescue

To easily lift a dish or a meat loaf out of the slow cooker, make foil handles according to the following directions.

Tear off three 18×3-inch strips of heavy-duty foil. Crisscross the strips so they resemble the spokes of a wheel. Place the dish or food in the center of the strips.

Pull the foil strips up and over the food and place it in the slow cooker. Leave the foil strips in the slow cooker while the dish is cooking. Use the foil to easily lift the food out when it has finished cooking.

Food Safety Tips

The best weapon against food contamination is organization. A clean and organized kitchen is more likely to be a safe kitchen.

Read the entire recipe before beginning, to ensure you have all the necessary ingredients and utensils.

It is a good idea to have two cutting boards. Use one for cutting raw meat, poultry and fish and the other for cutting fresh fruits, vegetables and other foods. Always wash cutting boards and utensils with hot, soapy water after each use.

If you do any advance preparation, such as trimming meat or cutting vegetables, refrigerate the food until you're ready to start cooking. Store food in resealable plastic food storage bags. To avoid cross-contamination, always place raw meat, poultry and fish on the lowest shelf in the refrigerator. Place fruits and vegetables on higher shelves or in a crisper drawer.

Once the dish has finished cooking, don't keep it in the slow cooker too long. Foods need to be kept cooler than 40°F or hotter than 140°F to avoid the growth of harmful bacteria. Remove food to a clean container, cover and refrigerate as soon as possible. Do not reheat leftovers in the slow cooker. Use a microwave oven, the range-top or the oven for reheating.

General Substitutions

If you don't have:	Use:
1 cup buttermilk	1 tablespoon lemon juice or vinegar plus milk to equal 1 cup (stir; let stand 5 minutes)
1 tablespoon cornstarch	2 tablespoons all-purpose flour or 2 teaspoons arrowroot
1 whole egg	2 egg yolks plus 1 teaspoon cold water
1 teaspoon vinegar	2 teaspoons lemon juice
1 cup whole milk	1 cup skim milk plus 2 tablespoons melted butter
1 cup sour cream	1 cup plain yogurt

Weights and Measures

Dash	=	Less than ⅛ teaspoon
½ tablespoon	=	1½ teaspoons
1 tablespoon	=	3 teaspoons
⅛ cup	=	2 tablespoons
¼ cup	=	4 tablespoons
⅓ cup	=	5 tablespoons plus 1 teaspoon
½ cup	=	8 tablespoons
¾ cup	=	12 tablespoons
1 cup	=	16 tablespoons
½ pint	=	1 cup or 8 fluid ounces
1 pint	=	2 cups or 16 fluid ounces
1 quart	=	4 cups or 2 pints or 32 fluid ounces
1 gallon	=	16 cups or 4 quarts or 128 fluid ounces
1 pound	=	16 ounces

Metric Conversion Chart

VOLUME MEASUREMENTS (dry)

1/8 teaspoon = 0.5 mL
1/4 teaspoon = 1 mL
1/2 teaspoon = 2 mL
3/4 teaspoon = 4 mL
1 teaspoon = 5 mL
1 tablespoon = 15 mL
2 tablespoons = 30 mL
1/4 cup = 60 mL
1/3 cup = 75 mL
1/2 cup = 125 mL
2/3 cup = 150 mL
3/4 cup = 175 mL
1 cup = 250 mL
2 cups = 1 pint = 500 mL
3 cups = 750 mL
4 cups = 1 quart = 1 L

VOLUME MEASUREMENTS (fluid)

1 fluid ounce (2 tablespoons) = 30 mL
4 fluid ounces (1/2 cup) = 125 mL
8 fluid ounces (1 cup) = 250 mL
12 fluid ounces (1 1/2 cups) = 375 mL
16 fluid ounces (2 cups) = 500 mL

WEIGHTS (mass)

1/2 ounce = 15 g
1 ounce = 30 g
3 ounces = 90 g
4 ounces = 120 g
8 ounces = 225 g
10 ounces = 285 g
12 ounces = 360 g
16 ounces = 1 pound = 450 g

DIMENSIONS

1/16 inch = 2 mm
1/8 inch = 3 mm
1/4 inch = 6 mm
1/2 inch = 1.5 cm
3/4 inch = 2 cm
1 inch = 2.5 cm

OVEN TEMPERATURES

250°F = 120°C
275°F = 140°C
300°F = 150°C
325°F = 160°C
350°F = 180°C
375°F = 190°C
400°F = 200°C
425°F = 220°C
450°F = 230°C

BAKING PAN SIZES

Utensil	Size in Inches/Quarts	Metric Volume	Size in Centimeters
Baking or Cake Pan (square or rectangular)	8×8×2	2 L	20×20×5
	9×9×2	2.5 L	23×23×5
	12×8×2	3 L	30×20×5
	13×9×2	3.5 L	33×23×5
Loaf Pan	8×4×3	1.5 L	20×10×7
	9×5×3	2 L	23×13×7
Round Layer Cake Pan	8×1½	1.2 L	20×4
	9×1½	1.5 L	23×4
Pie Plate	8×1¼	750 mL	20×3
	9×1¼	1 L	23×3
Baking Dish or Casserole	1 quart	1 L	—
	1½ quart	1.5 L	—
	2 quart	2 L	—

Index

Index

Index

Index

Index

Index

Index